Decomposed Woman

Hamide Mirzad

Hamide Mirzad was born in Herat, Afghanistan. After escaping from Afghanistan she experienced a period of living in Iran, before emigrating to Norway in 2008. Three collections of poetry and a novel have already been published by this author. Hamide has also worked on two other projects, both collections of poems by other Persian-speaking poets, released in 2019 and 2020. She is currently a student at the University of Oslo.

1. I want to die standing up (collections of poetry)
   Author: Hamide Mirzad
   Publisher: Amiri Publications 2014(Afghanistan)
   Language: Persian

2. One drop left to become the sea (collections of poetry)
   Author Name: Hamide Mirzad
   Publisher: Young Poetry House, 2016, Afghanistan
   Language: Persian

3. The dark half of a dream (roman)
   Author: Hamide Mirzad
   ISBN: 978 1985243194
   Publisher: Nebesht 2018
   Language: Persian

4. Yellow fuss (collections of poetry)
   Author: Hamide Mirzad
   Published: First, 1399
   ISBN: 9-22-657-9936-978
   Publisher: An, Afghanistan
   Language: Persian

Copyright © 2022 by Hamide Mirzad

All rights reserved. No part of this publication may be reproduced, stored in any form of retrieval system or transmitted in any form or by any means without prior permission in writing from the publishers except for the use of brief quotations in a book review.

ISBNs:
Paperback: 978-1-80227-307-6
eBook: 978-1-80227-308-3

Contents

Chapter 1 5
Chapter 2 8
Chapter 3 15
Chapter 4 24
Chapter 5 31
Chapter 6 57
Chapter 7 71
Chapter 8 97
Chapter 9 121
Chapter 10 132

Chapter 1

The legs of the chair had started to creak because she was so restless; she just couldn't keep still. Sometimes she bunched her hands into fists, she would twist them together, and other times she would clutch her head between her hands in sheer frustration. Her black and bold eyes were damp from tears. The deep, dark circles beneath them were evidence of the sleeplessness of the previous night.

The consultant, a middle-aged woman, talked slowly, "how do you feel today?"

As she stared at the picture in her line of sight, she answered: "just like always, how should I feel?"

The consultant followed her patient's gaze and said, "this picture was created by one of my patients who came to me for a consultation. Do you have a favorite form of art, that you enjoy?

As she continued to stare at the picture, she said, "they're dead".

Consultant, "who?"

"I'm talking about my desires - they all died with him."

As an impartial witness, I had no right to speak, I was only there to translate their conversations. Sometimes the talk was combined with moaning, and that made what was said unclear and difficult to translate. She got angry if I asked her to repeat anything.

I moved the bottle of water on the table toward her and said "relax!". She became calmer after drinking and started talking again. In a short period of time, the relief was gone, and quickly replaced by crying and anger. Shethumped her fist down hard on the table in the middle of the room, then moved towards the door. I grabbed her shoulder, so she wouldn't fall, but she angrily distanced herself from me and continued to walk towards the exit without saying anything. The consultant said in an apologetic manner, that today was not a good day for talking. I didn't know what to do. All my attention was on the woman. She hit herself again as she tried to leave; she was like a caged bird trying to escape. She wanted to leave the room. My sympathy for her predicament made me want to cry, but I made every effort not to do so.

When the consultant saw the extent of anxiety of her patient she said, "that's enough for today".

She wrote a date on the yellow appointment card and handed it to me. It was the date of the next meeting, which I took to give to the woman's escort. I followed her out of the room and saw a young boy who was guiding her and helping her to put on her coat.

After greeting him, I handed the yellow appointment card to him and said, "the doctor wrote the date of the next meeting on this card and asked me to give it to you".

He interrupted me and said, "she is my mother".

I said, "yes, I hope that she be better soon. If there's anything I can do, any favor, I would be only too happy to help".

He smiled gently and said, "thanks for your sympathy."

***

In the dark and cold days of winter, the face of a foreign land becomes clearer than ever. The shadows of war followed my people to the cold roads of northern Europe. My job was closely linked to the bitter fate of my people, like I was present in the lives of all of them. Sometimes the bitter destiny of the mentally ill patients or the delinquent juveniles increased my nightmares. Although I loved my job, and I kept my connection with my

Roots, I knew what was going on in my country, and how deep my fellow citizens' pains were.

On another day when I was again called to the psychiatric clinic, to be a translator for a meeting. I saw that same mother and son again.

The young man greeted me and said, "I am Vahid, and my mother's name is Roya. I asked the doctor to have you as our permanent translator. could you please help us with that".

I said, "that's okay, I will do anything in my power to help".

For six months I was with Roya in every psychotherapy session she had, but her situation never changed. Her sad eyes reflected the depth of her loneliness. She barely talked, cried a lot, and got angry very easily.

At the end of one of consultation session, Vahid requested a private meeting.

The doctor asked Vahid, "what do you know about your mother's life? For example, her childhood, or adolescence?"

He said, "I don't know so much, but my mother has a diary which is never separated from her".

The consultant asked, "does she still write in her diary?"

Vahid answered, "I never saw her write anything in it".

The consultant said, "since Roya is not in a good situation, the law gives us permission to read the diary. Maybe it will help diagnose Roya's illness. That would allow us to give her more effective treatment".

It was decided that Vahid would deliver the diary to the mental health team. I would get the diary in a few days. I would then read it and translate it for them. I was impatiently looking forward to getting home to study that old diary inside which Roya's life was hidden. I wanted to know what events had made such a deep impression on her, causing the silence and destroying her soul little by little. When I got home, I didn't stop to do anything else; I went straight to my bag and opened the sorrows and joys of Roya on the table.

Chapter 2

I couldn't help but stare in surprise, eyes open wide – there was a very big yard, green gardens, trees with colorful fruits, and spacious rooms covered with red Afghan carpets. After the poverty and misery of my grandfather's house, this new home was like something from a distant dream for me. As I washed my muddy and cracked legs beside the turquoise fountain in the yard, I watched the fishes idly swimming in the water. I thought, joyfully, this is finally our home. My face got hot in the sunlight. I was playing with my dark plaited hair, daydreaming, when the rough and tough voice of Hadji brought me abruptly back to reality. – I was like a little bird trapped in a golden cage.

"What are you staring at, girl? Go and help your mother. We have guests."

Suddenly a big sadness mocked my small joy. Disarranged ideas attacked my imagination, like a wolf stealing an innocent white lamb. In my mind, I was replaying the conversation between my grandfather and my mother. I thought I might find answers to my questions in their words.

"My girl, you are a beautiful and educated woman, but this beauty won't always be with you. That god-blessed man who talked of being open-minded, died and left you and me with this orphan girl. You've been rejecting all suitors for your hand for two years now. I ask you to accept. Hadji Rasool's proposal and release me from this responsibility."

"Dear sir, I can't accept this man as that blessed one."

"I understand, my daughter. Your husband was a great man, he left this world and now you are alone. I can't take responsibility for you and yourdaughter any further. Hadji Gholam Rasoul has a good reputation, and everyone respects him. Half of the lands of Zende Jan belong to him. Hispoor wife, died during the birth of his last child. Until now, when his children are grown, he still hasn't married again."

"Dear father, I know Hadji Rasoul is a wealthy man. But he is also a hard-headed and radical man; his mindset is very different from mine. He is responsible for the death of his wife because he didn't allow her to be taken to hospital during childbirth. It is clear as day that Hadji's house will be the shambles of me and Roya. But it seems you will coerce me into this no matter what I say. I can see it is useless to argue, so for your convenience I will accept his proposal."

"Well done, my daughter. I wish you a fortunate life."

During this same period, Hafizollah Amin was murdered in a coup, and Babrak Karmel replaced him. Military interference from the Soviet Union in Afghanistan became a disaster for its army; One hundred and fifty thousand soviet soldiers were maintained in Afghanistan. Hadji' Rasoul's house was also under political conflict. Hadji and his sons opposed this coup and didn't confirm last year's actions. A significant number of meetings were held in Hadji's office. Although Hadji Rasoul wasn't an educated man, he had learned enough political tricks to get him by. As quoted by himself, 'he who throws his money under the sun, sits down in the shadow[1]. Amid war and crisis, he had made some people his slaves and represented himself as a master. What crimes he did under the cover of politics shouldn't be mentioned, nor should what huge benefits he acquired while fishing in troubled waters.

---

[1] An old Persian saying meaning he uses his money to make more money, without using physical strength.

My childhood contained my mother's pain and suffering. I had lost the joy and happiness in the noise of weapons and cannon-fire. Sometimes we went to a relative's house, to escape from the pursuit of hadji's political opponents. Taher took hold of my plaited hair and forced me to go with him. Taher and Zaher were almost the same age, and they were very tall. They had lovely faces while they were smiling. They always tried to copy their father's behavior, maybe because they didn't have a better role model. You could see the anger of Gholam Rasoulin the young face of Taher, and his tough talking in Zaher's voice. Gholam Rasoul was a complete contrast to my dead father. He called my father a pagan. Without knowing the meaning of it, it was pronounced in a way that its negative meaning weighed heavily like a mountain on my shoulders.

***

By the time I was fifteen I had spent seven years witnessing the abasement of my mother in Hadji's house. Seeing guns on the shoulders of Hadji and his sons, became common. Children playing on the abandoned hulks of Russian tanks that had been destroyed, and the goodbyes of migrating neighbors, were among our daily routines. During these years, the Democratic Party was defeated in Afghanistan. Soviet's red army, despite killing more than one million Afghans, didn't win against the Mujaheddin. The Russians eventually left Afghanistan, but unfortunately, different groups of Mujaheddin fought each other for official positions. Today, Hadji and his sons had been fighting against their former comrades. Meanwhile, only the situation of my mother and myself hadn't changed. We were prisoners who had to work hard.

Hard work at Hadji Rasoul's house, and the '120-day winds' of Herat[2] have made my feminine soft skin, dry and broken. I took a small container of Vaseline from my scarf and dabbed a little on my cheeks. The image reflected in the smoky mirror in the kitchen, showed that I was now a teenager. The kitchen was the only place in the house that hadn't been modernized and had kept its traditional style. Somehow it seemed like that kitchen was not a part of this big house. Unfortunately, my mother and I spent long hours of the day in this disappointing and smoky kitchen. The corners of the walls were full of our whines.

I took the tray with the cups on it to the guestroom. I hadn't entered the room when I heard the conversation between Hadji and my mother. I placed my ear against the door to hear better.

Hadji said, "tomorrow, Azim's mother comes to ask for your daughter's hand in marriage".

Mother replied, "man, please have some sense of justice; that man has a wife and child, how can I send my dear girl to his house?"

Hadji replied, "he is a wealthy and powerful man. Your daughter will be happy, and I will get rid of my debts".

My mother said, "so you want to settle your large debt with my daughter as payment?"

When I heard this conversation, my legs froze, and my hands shook. The tray slipped from my hands and the sound of cups breaking combined with Hadji's rough voice.

"There is no benefit in keeping that useless girl. I've paid out for her upkeep for a long time, and now I should reap some of the benefits. Shouldn't I?"

---

[2] The 120-day winds of Herat refers to the season of strong winds particular to this area.

I was making fresh tea when I felt mother's hand on my shoulder. She wanted to inform me about tomorrow's proposal.

I said, "I heard everything," and threw myself into her arms. My mother had protected me many times, saving me from unwanted marriages. Hadji had insisted on my marriage for many years. Sometimes he wanted to trade me for a vehicle, sometimes to trade me for property. Mother opposed it every time and rejected the proposals with various excuses. She was always heavily beaten throughout these conflicts.

"Maybe I can stop this marriage, too". I felt relaxed within the comforting circle of my mother's sympathy.

Later I sat at the dinner table, the many fears I had going around and around in my head. Hadji and his sons were sat on one side, while me, mother, Pouran and Parvin, my half-sisters, were on the other side.

My mother started talking and said to Hadji with huge doubt in her voice, "if you agree, I'll sell my gold to pay Azim's debt". She hadn't even finished talking when the bowl of food hit her head and the controversy started.

"Why do you always have to disagree with me? Every year, you say she is young yet, and not ready for marriage. Now she is fifteen, you want to 'make pickle from her[3]'?"

My mother gathered bits of pea and potato from her clothes where the bowl of food had hit her and said with tears, "make her a bride, but not to a married man, not against your debt. You are not looking to marry her; you want to sell her?"

Zaher said, instead of Hadji, "what's the difference? She should marry. What's the difference whether it's for father's debt, or money or a vehicle!".

---

[3] Pickles is an obscene term in Persian culture that is used for girls who are older and have not married.

Taher continued, "it is always war with this girl in the house. If she goes, we'll all feel more relaxed".

My mother didn't reply, it seemed that she knew this time she would lose. She went to her room to change her clothes. I cleaned the table and went after her. She was sad and crying. Seeing her like that, for one second, I decided to accept any condition. Maybe then she would be calmer.

I sat beside her and said, "don't cry. Let this marriage be done; I am tired of these conflicts".

Mother's sad eyes touched my disappointed face. She hugged me and said "I didn't keep my responsibilities towards you. I'm sorry".

I said, "you tried your hardest; I don't want you to suffer any more for me".

I slept that night in my mother's kind arms, looking towards a darker tomorrow. The next day, suitors came as Hadji had promised. Azim's mother was an exceptionally ugly woman. She had green moles that seemed to erupt from under her wrinkled face. When I saw her, I started shaking unconsciously. I said to myself, 'it is done this time, may God save me'. Suddenly the voice of the old woman distracted my thoughts.

"Come, come my dear bride, my son has good taste. We made a deal on a good object."

My mother looked at me sorrowfully and led me by the hand to sit beside the old lady. She took my hand and as the others whispered to each other, she placed a ring on my finger. What should I do? I rejected the old lady's hand and gave her an angry glare as I ran towards the door. I tried to go out into the yard, but a hand prevented me from going. She and her sons were making sure the deal was finished. Hadji slapped me hard on the ear. Then Zaher grabbed me by the hair and dragged me toward the guestroom. The ring was on my finger, like a rope on a slave's neck.

I couldn't do anything to help myself. I felt defeated. I had no place between the living or the dead. I was someone in the middle. I was alive, because I moved, walked, and worked. Dead because of the frustration and helplessness. To escape from the unwanted future created by others, I conjured up a thousand plans in my head, but got no results. My pillow that night was soaked with my tears. I wished I would never wake up again.

Chapter 3

The black hair of my sister, Parvin, was in my one hand, and the comb in the other hand, as I played with both. I was drowning in my sorrowful thoughts. Sometimes a few drops of tears wetted my eye.

Parvin was tired of sitting beside me, and she asked, "why don't you get on and braid my hair? I'm getting tired of this".

I said I was sorry. Was Parvin's future as dark as mine? Whose house would she be sent into? But no. Hadji's blood was in Parvin's veins, so he might not do the same to his own daughter. She would end up happy – her future was bright. She was only four years old then, and everything could change by the time she grew up.

My mother disrupted my thoughts. She said, "Azim has travelled to Kandahar. When he returns, maybe we'll have your wedding".

In a moment, the fearful face of my future owner passed through my mind. His angry eyes made me shudder.

I said to my mother, "I wish I had never been born a girl. Being a woman means being powerless, abasement, humiliation. And by the way, mother, you knew our situation in this house. So, why did you let Parvin and Pouran be born?"

She said, "it was not up to me. Hadji wanted children, and for many years the voice of a child wasn't heard in this house".

"Even in the birth of your children, you were nothing more than a womb to him. I don't want to be treated like this. Please do me a favor."

"We can't do anything, anymore; you are chosen for him".

Hearing this sentence was like emptying a bucket of cold water over my head. I said, "but you claimed that you satisfied your husband?".

She said with tears in her eyes, "you saw how much I was beaten for this? I can't tolerate anymore". She exploded and cried continuously. "Every part of my body is bruised, I am in such pain, I can't tolerate it anymore, I haven't had one good day since I married Hadji. Since you've grown up, he's found excuse after excuse for hurting me. It is your destiny my girl. You can't escape it. Women can't choose in this country". My mother's words were like an iron hammer hitting my head. I couldn't accept it. Would I be someone like my mother? A victim, a failed person with cracked hands and permanently tear-filled eyes?

It was the picture of my future, moving in front of my eyes. She would pay for the silence, but I wasn't going to accept such a destiny. I always dreamed that someday, I would leave this house and land in a more fortunate situation. My future was shattered and disappeared in the glimpse of an eye. What could I say in response to my mother? She was right, too. She was tired. I bowed my head and was silent.

It was past midnight. The face of my mother, sleeping, so very tired and desperate like the moon, reflected the horrible future in my head. I was looking for an escape. But how? From what? To where? A thousand locked doors were in front of me. I needed to accept this life that was being forced on me or say goodbye to life. Every second that passed, I became more eager. Indeed, I wanted to finish this forceful life. It was better for everyone. My mother wouldn't have an unfortunate daughter to cry for. I wouldn't be forced towards this misery. Slowly, this thought became dominant in my mind. Facing death was the first and last solution.

That night, I didn't sleep until morning. When I got up, I went into the kitchen to prepare tea. A new thought suddenly appeared to my mind. It was like my inner identity ordered me to do this. I didn't know what would happen. I emptied a gallon of petrol on my head and lit a match. In no time, I was in a mass of flames. I didn't understand anything else. Every piece of the unfortunate events that led to this, passed from my mind like a tragic film. I only heard the screams of my mother and perceived nothing more.

***

I gathered all my energy to open my eyes. My body was burning, and I remembered what I had done to myself. All my upper body was bandaged. Mother was beside my bed.

When she realized I was awake, she said "are you awake? Thank God for returning you to me. If Saeid hadn't been there, I couldn't have saved you on my own. If that butcher had been in the house, you would have been burnt to death. He wouldn't have allowed you to be taken to the hospital – his precious reputation would have been threatened because of your suicide attempt". When Saeid's mother arrived, it stopped my mother's conversation. She was a lovely woman. She kissed me and reflected contentment because I was alive.

When I asked about Saeid's situation, she paused for a few seconds and said, "he is around here somewhere; his face and hands have small injuries which should be taken care of".

I said, "I am sorry, I caused you trouble".

She said, "no, you are like my daughter".

In the meantime, Saeid entered the room. He looked tired and affected. His hands were burnt a little. He stood by my bed and asked, "do you feel better?"

I said, "thanks to you". But I wish I had died in the flames, so that I turned to ashes.

The visit ended. My family and friends left. It was me with a burned body and heart in way worse pain. Why was I alive? I wanted to free myself from this misery. Why? The world was limited for me. I wanted to destroy this cage that is my body, so that my soul could fly freely. Who could I talk to? I didn't want to live with abasement. My hands needed help, but where was a kind and capable hand to take my hand? How many silent cries should I tolerate? I was tired, very tired.

One week had passed since I had been hospitalized. Meanwhile I saw so much misery in the people there, my sadness worsened: dirty and crowded rooms, sick children, sad mothers, night cries - it all broke me. I forgot my own sadness amongst that of all the others. In the night, it was me with this humongous lump of fear and sadness. My eyes were fixated at a corner. A fearful nightmare of my future wouldn't leave me alone. Sadness and frustration followed me like a ghost. Where could I go to escape? As soon as I left the hospital, I would be sent to my husband's house, and everything would be over. I had hurt their reputation. I had to marry soon, so they could face the neighbors.

It was morning again, and it was a new start to my miseries. It was around 10.00 am that my mother, Saeid and his mother came to see me. Mother asked how I was, and Lady Faezeh pressed my hand as warmly as ever.

She said, "how are you?" I hadn't answered yet when she said, "I couldn't stop Saeid today; he was worried about you and came with us".

Then Saeid started talking and asked me, "how are you".

I couldn't look at him and said, "not bad, alive thanks to you".

He continued, "my sisters, Lina and Leyla said hello; they're looking for your return.

I said, "tell them I said hello".

There was no further discussion. the nurse entered and said, "how do you feel, Roya dear? Are you ready for me to take off the bandage on your face?".

I said, "can we leave it for one more day?"

I didn't want Saeid to see my burnt face. The nurse ignored my request and started removing the bandage anyway. When she had finished, I understood from my mother's astonished face how terrible I must look.

She screamed and said, "see what a disaster you have made of yourself. What will I do with you?"

Saeid was worried but tried to calm my mother down. She was still crying but wiped her eyes with a corner of her Hijab. Lady Faezeh had tears running down her fat cheeks, but she also helped calm my mother.

The nurse said, "dear mother, thank God! Her facial scars aren't deep. Only her skin is burnt. I assure you that her past beauty will return very soon. The scars are new and because of that they seem worse than they really are".

I was shocked at that moment. I couldn't tolerate any more. I put my head under the blanket and cried very loudly. I cried for my dark and unfortunate destiny. I screamed, "I don't want to be here, I don't want to be alive? Why? Why I am alive?"

Meanwhile a hand angrily snatched the blanket from off my head. My eyes investigated his angry face.

He said, "you don't want to be alive? You are a coward, running away from your problems? If you are a brave woman, fight for your right. Fight! Crying and screaming only show your weakness".

I didn't get a chance to reply before he said, "don't say anything, just think about my words". Then he looked at my mother and said, "let's go".

Saeid was an educated man, raised in a family of great culture. Their house was at the end of our alley. A small house, but its residents had big hearts. Faezeh had two daughters and one son. Saeid studied at The Faculty of Law. Both of his sisters studied at Leese school. Lina was my classmate when we were both still young. We were very close to each.

other. Hadji Rasoul always talked badly about them. He said, "their daughters are adults, but still go to school".

He got me out of school at ten, and said, "you are grown up. It is not appropriate. It is time for your wedding."

Sometimes I asked Lina to lend her books to me, in secret. Thanks to her, I slowly studied at home. And now thanks to her brother's favor I had escaped death.

Night-time was approaching the window. The red sunset of Herat was very beautiful. It was red like the blood, of innocent people being killed every day. It was like all that blood was spread in the sky. That night, my tolerance was broken, and my cries blocked my throat. I had no power for crying anymore. Every second that was passing was like a century. The occasional coughs of an old woman in my ward, kept me awake. Then I sunk into my isolation, like a canary bird in a cage.

The door of the ward opened, and I saw Saeid entering the room. I thought I was dreaming. It was night, what was he doing here?

He came forward and asked, "are you better?"

I turned my face away from him and said, "why did you come? Why put yourself in danger? Don't you know my family? They won't show mercy".

He laughed and said, "Hadji and his sons went to Kandahar. Your mother is alone and needs help. I came here to take your news to her".

I said, "well, you have given the information; now you can

leave". He said, "why do you turn your face away?"

I said angrily, "what do you want to see? The mark of patriarchy? The mark of dirty tradition? Dear sir, you should know that one action won't change anything; you are one against thousands? What do you want to change? If they find out you are here and not a family member, they will attack you and beat you up".

He said ironically, "if you want them to, tell them", And then continued, "Lina said you are very interested in reading. Let useless ideas go, read this book". He put a book beside my bed and after a few seconds I heard the door close, but I turned my face away and didn't see him leave.

His words and concern invited me to a new challenge. I looked up towards the heavens, and said, "God, you know I am constrained by tradition. What is this test you have set for me?". I ignored the whisper of my heart; reached out and took the book - on the cover it was written "Hafez Shirazi". I opened it. On the first page, it was written:

'In disappointment, there is a lot of hope

the end of the dark night is light.'

And it was signed, Saeid.

The poem injected new energy into every vessel of my body. In the anxiety of my heart I thought, 'what is this familiar sound, which persuades me to hope'? I wasn't very familiar with the writings of Hafez. I had heard his name from my teacher and Lina a few times. I remembered Lina once said, 'we sit together at night, and understand our prophecy through Hafez's book'. I made a wish and opened a page. This beautiful tradition that Hafez wrote appeared on the page in front of me:

The day of remoteness and night of separation ended.

I made this prophecy, and the star passed, and the job got done.

I took an optimistic view of this and slept calmer than the previous nights. I had a strange feeling, a feeling I had never experienced before.

I watched myself in the mirror. My face was pink and not like my usual self at all. This time I didn't get sad, and I said to myself, 'be strong and fight'. Fight was a word I had heard many times over the years, but only from people such as Hadji and his sons. But now Saeid had given this word a whole new meaning.

I spent another ten days at the hospital. Saeid came to see me every night. His calm face and beautiful voice healed my heart. I saw myself being a free bird, that was just beginning to get familiar with the idea. My luck was changing for the better. Maybe I could settle into a more fortunate place through his powerful wings.

I was satisfied that despite bitter problems, and by tolerating them, I could savor the sweet taste of felicity. He gave me the strength to fight the forceful conditions of my life, with the highest power. He read Hafez to me every night, and washed my disappointments away, as if the words were like clear and flowing water. His kind look made me calm. In all these nights, I never had a bad feeling about him, even once. He was a gentleman – that much was evident.

The night before my release, I was very sad. I told Saeid that I would go home in the morning.

He answered, "very well, thank God".

I asked, "are you not upset?"

He replied, "does anyone get sad when their friend is returned to good health? Are you sad?"

I said, "tomorrow is the beginning to my misery. as soon as I return to the house, Azim and his family will ask Hadji about their prize".

He said, "once more, you are worrying, and thinking about death. Don't be afraid, I am with you". With that conversation, I knew that I wasn't alone anymore.

I slept that night comfortably, anticipating a busy day tomorrow. That morning after my release from the hospital, we traveled home with my mother and lady Faezeh, from my part with a lot of horror and fear. My little sisters, Pouran and Parvin, were very excited when they saw me. They hugged me while crying and asked, "why are you like this?

I had no answer to their questions. I asked my mother, "when will Hadji and his sons return?"

She said, "it is not clear when they will come. Perhaps they return today or tomorrow".

In the afternoon, Faezeh and her daughters came to see me. Lina gave me a book from Saeid, when no one else was around.

The first three days were good. Lina and Leyla came to our house every day. We enjoyed sweet conversations together. At night, after studying, I slept comfortably. I wished all of my family was this sweet and happy, then I wouldn't have to try to end my life.

Chapter 4

I was awoken in the morning by mother's voice, "Roya, Roya, wake up! I think the boys came home last night". I was still rubbing the sleep off my eyes, when all three came to my room like wolves.

I said, "hello".

Hadji showed his anger saying "hello you venomous, fatherless girl. You have destroyed our reputation, made over the years. Because of your wrongful action, we had to go away."

I just cried.

Suddenly Zaher took me by the hair. He made me stand up and shouted, "you are shameless! You don't know anything about dignity. We don't want you here anymore. Leave our house!"

My mother said through her tears, "where will she go? She has no one except me. Please leave her alone".

Taher replied angrily, "you always defend her. this happened because of your support. This time she has to go."

Hadji said to his sons, "leave her, I will finish the job today".

He left still growling to himself. When they left, it seemed that the huge storm in our house had ended. I anxiously told my mother about Saeid coming to the hospital. She listened to me with surprise and an open mouth. Sometimes she bit her lips. It was like I had committed a huge crime.

Finally, she said with fear in her voice, "if you won't save yourself, at least think about him; they will hurt him for sure. You don't know how much blood other young people have shed in this situation. On the otherhand, you are chosen for Hadji Azim - your father has left to make the wedding arrangements".

I cried, "didn't you say you would stop this? So, what happened?"

She said "I can't. There is not an inch of my body without bruises. It is your destiny, accept it. This is Afghanistan. Only a few of fortunate women can make decisions about their lives. You and I are not part of them. Accept your destiny and see what happens."

The voice of my stepfather stopped us from speaking.

"Roya, where are you? Tomorrow, Azim's family come for the scarf and ring ceremony, this time you will neither bother your mother, nor destroy our reputation. Let the plans go ahead without any trouble. We are all tired."

The face of Azim was summoned in front of my eyes, and the fear of my future shook my body. I spent that night sick with fear of what tomorrow would bring. Desire was dead inside me. Mother combed my hair, which was wet with my tears, and put new clothes on me. But her effort to cover the scars on my face were useless. I was waiting in the corner of the room for my buyers, like a statue. I would be given to them without any objection. I was going to be drowned in the swamp of my destiny.

Gradually, the guests arrived. The song of me being sacrificed echoed in my ears. Expensive gifts were brought, but amongst them all, I only saw Azim's angry face. After chai tea and cookies[4], the groom's mother came to me, to give me her expensive gift. She was going to name me for her son. But when she drew closer she stared at me in shocked surprise.

---

[4] In Afghanistan good news is celebrated with the buying and eating of sweet things.

She said to my mother, "is this the same girl, or are you playing us?"

Mother said, "a few days ago, there was a fire in the kitchen and my girl was injured, but she will be well again very soon".

She said, "Hadji Azim didn't have a deal on a burnt girl. We don't want her."

Hadji, who had been sitting outside in the yard until the ceremony finished, heard the commotion and said, "hello" and entered women's room.

He said, "what happened? Why are you shouting mother?"

The groom's mother said to us, "I couldn't see in the beginning; I didn't see your girl had been burned. I know my son doesn't want her, so you better think about paying your debt". Then she gathered her family together and they stalked out angrily taking with them all the gifts that they had brought.

I was very happy to have escaped from this situation, in my heart. I was laughing at the twists and turns of destiny. I remembered Saeid's words, 'don't make it worse, before death'.

My mother came to me and while laughing, calmly said, "thank God it ended, let's go! You should change your clothes".

Hadji screamed and said, "what shall I do with my debt to Azim now?"

He swore at me and my mother. After a lot of pushes and pulls, I was sent to the small outhouse on the other side of the yard. I was thrown into the darkness there. The door was closed, and I was locked in. It was just me, alone with all my sorrows, the sadness of being an orphan.

Destiny was like a wild horse, and I was linked to its tail. Sometimes it moved slowly, sometimes very fast so that I was smashed to the rocks and fainted from severe pain. That night, without paying attention to past and future sadness, and any kind of seen and unseen conflict, I looked toward unlimited events. I didn't know where they were taking me.

How could I break free from my fears? I should be eager to end these bitter years. But with what power? After such damaging events, nobody wanted me or came forward for me. Finally, the door opened. I couldn't see in the dazzling light after the darkness of my confinement. I didn't know who was coming for me. Are they going to hurt me again? When whoever it was drew closer, I knew it was my mother who came to see me. She sat beside me and said, "how are you, my daughter?".

I was silent, just crying. She took care of my scars and bandaged them again.

I said, "I wish I was dead, so you'd be free of all this conflict".

She said, "my girl, death is not a good solution, stand your ground and fight". I never forgot her eyes. Frustrated eyes and cracked hands, pale skin and slender cheeks, all directing me towards crying. She pressed my hand warmly and sympathized with me. She put the food in my mouth, piece by piece. My mother's lap was the safest place for me. But each day, when Hadji came home, she hurried away and returned to him.

I lost count of the days. Day and night were the same for me. Both were dark and black. I thought about how to leave this place but couldn't find any solution. I was broken and had lost half of my life.

Then one day Hadji came to me and said, "you can come out now, but remember this - never disobey us, or we will bury you here".

I was shaking, but I said nothing and limped out of that prison and back to my mother.

My mother helped me and sent me to my room. I looked like I'd been many years in prison. I was very pale. My hair was scruffy. I bathed with the help of mother.

She put a mirror in my hand and said, "your face is better, don't worry anymore, the cream I used on it was given to me by Saeid's mother; their brother sent it from abroad. God bless them, they asked about you every day."

I interrupted my mother's talk and said "what about Saeid? Where is he?"

She said "I asked him not to come here. He told his mother that he wanted you - they will come soon to make a proposal".

After a long time, a smile appeared on my lips. This news healed my injuries. I was optimistic about life during that time. The beautiful face of Saeid sent me into the world of dreams. I accepted his kind notes brought to me by Lina. I accepted the soft emotions that washed over me, body and soul, I was in tears at so much kindness. I woke up happy every day and did the chores eagerly. The skin on my face had healed completely and incredibly, I heard from the doctor that keeping me in the dark of the outhouse and preventing sunlight from entering for such a long time had been a huge help in healing my scars.

I was looking for the bird of happiness to come to me once more, and give me unlimited contentment under her wing. My only concern was that it might all be a dream. And when I woke up in the morning, I'd see the pieces of my dreams shattered all over the floor. I looked toward indefinite space, in order to find my wishes.

One day, early in the morning, my eyes focused on something else when I opened the door. My instinctive feeling said they had come to make a proposal. I found myself in Faezeh's arms and after kissing and greeting I said, "please come inside, my mother is there".

I led them in, anxious from head to toe, I made tea very quickly. After serving tea, I left the room, but my childish curiosity, wouldn't leave me alone. I walked very slowly toward the door and tried to hear their conversation.

Saeid's mother said, "we are here with good intentions. If you allow us, we will return with our family between one and one hundred days from now".

My mother answered, "feel at home, but let me ask her father; you know his behavior".

Leyla said, "it is necessary that you should consult with him. You talk tonight and we will return for his answer in the morning".

After a lot more conversation the suitors were ready to leave, Faezeh hugged me and slowly whispered in my ear, "my dear bride, I wish you good fortune".

Happiness! I was unfamiliar with it, maybe it was white, like a bridal veil with white context and flowers. Mother and daughter, we were united in our happiness.

Mother said, "your fortune has brightened with a good person."

I smiled and said, "but I am concerned about Hadji! He might refuse to allow it.

Mother replied, "leave it in the hands of God."

At night, after dinner, mother put a cup of tea in front of Hadji. She addressed him fearfully, "today, a suitor came for Roya".

Hadji and his sons looked at me together and asked, "who was he?"

Hadji continued, "what is their economic condition? From which family? Can they pay the gift we determine?" Everything was asked except the job and the education of the boy. My mother answered, "the son of Zabihollah, the draper, our neighbor at the end of the alley."

Hadji said angrily, "why should I care about education? Poor people don't have anything else and follow education, they forget honor and leave their girls in the alleys".

Mother looked at me desperately and asked Hadji, "well, what answer should I give them?"

He said, "when they come in the morning, I will give them the answer myself".

A huge sadness appeared in my heart. I knew that hugging Saeid was going to be impossible. I slept that night tossing and turning with a lot of worry. In the morning, I was very concerned about what answer Hadji would give to Saeid's proposal.

Hearing knocking, my heart started beating wildly. I looked over at the window towards Hadji, who was going to open the door. Seeing Faezeh on the doorstep, I got even more anxious, and my heartbeatdoubled. I strained my ears to hear what was said.

After saying hello, Hadji started talking without further delay and said, "I know you have come for my answer. You are our neighbor, but you should know your place. There is a huge distance between us. If you care about your son's life, look for a daughter like yourself…, end of story".

Faezeh tried to speak, "but…."

Hadji stopped her right there and said, "goodbye," and closed the door in her face.

A cry was in my throat. I wouldn't be able to look at Saeid and his family anymore. I desperately moved towards my mother and as always, I emptied my tears on her sorrow-laden shoulder.

I begged my mother, "will you help me? I will die without Saeid. Help me to turn this around".

She said, "my daughter, please be patient; believe in God. Time will resolve everything. Of course, I will help, but at the right time and that has not yet arrived."

Chapter 5

In the summer of 1995, Herat fell to Taliban after a dark and chaotic night. The Taliban appeared in the bloody land like shrubs and took the power to themselves. It was an adventurous period. Hadji Rasoul couldn't be calm because of his intense anger. He walked and nagged at it.

"It's so weird; the commanders of the Herat forces, who managed to fight off the Soviet Union, with all their battle experience - how can they have been so easily defeated by teachers of religion? They must have been supported by Pakistani forces. What should we do?"

A weird throbbing seemed to emanate from the city. Movement of women in the alleys and markets was almost zero. Girl's schools, female bathrooms and radio and TV centers were closed. Photographers and sculptors became criminals. Those people who had money and capital migrated to foreign countries, while the common people continued living under the shadow of misery and abasement.

Hadji and his sons were still among the warriors who claimed to be patriots and didn't like to flee. They followed the Taliban's rules so as not to being arrested. They travelled to different cities as vehicle service providers and helped the jihadists. They weren't home for weeks and months and this gave my mother and I an opportunity to improve our conditions. My relationship with Saeid's family became stronger.

Leyla, who was a teacher before the Taliban era, became isolated in the house. When all their hopes for the restoration of opening the schools again faded away, some parents asked Leyla to teach their children. Despite huge objections from Lady Faezeh, Leyla turned the basement into a secret school.

This decision was a big risk, but there was only one way to educate the girls.

In that time, Herat had become a city of violence and fear. Many of its citizens were looking for an escape. But Leyla stayed. And with help from myself and Lina, we taught the girls in the basement. Some girls came from our alley and the next alley, and we started teaching. There were younger and older students. They were so eager to learn and came despite the risk. In the early days we only had ten students. But every day their number increased. Teaching was accomplished in two shifts. Lina and I taught classes 1 to 4 pm, and Leyla taught the higher-level classes. We worked in the basement, where it was sort of dark.

We were all worried about the safety and life of the children. Students came with fear and stress, and at the end of each session, Saeid stood by the door and made sure that nobody was around as they stepped back out into the street, one or two children at a time.

The number of students rose to fifty. When I wasn't teaching, I was one of Leyla's students. During Leyla's lessons, I did my 'homework about love' towards Saeid. I was always the last student to leave the class.

Some days I had dates with Saeid. My body and soul wanted him so much. His manly shoulders were a good place to rest my head. I breathed for hours in his arms. He touched me and the joy kept me going until the next time we met.

Two years passed like this. With the help of Leyla, I finished tenth grade. Now I could easily answer Saeid's warm letters. My love for Saeid was so much that separation from him was like a death.

My mother knew about almost everything. She guided me like a kind friend. She said "my daughter, your dreams are logical, but try not to lose sight of your holy goals by committing sins. Be free but remain decent."

My mother's words were wise and beautiful but didn't have a place in love. Love was not guilt for me. Every day, I wanted the presence of Saeid more than ever. He was more attracted than ever and wanted every chance to be alone with me.

He said, "the days I don't have you is like I'm missing the most valuable thing in life. Always be with me, always".

I woke up another day with the sound of prayer. I went to the mosque asusual and cleaned myself. Praying was mandatory in Hadji's house, and Iwas used to it. I returned to bed, wondering if I could I ever be together with Saeid, and would I ever have a peaceful life with him?

The sound of a commotion took me out to the yard, my mother following me. I was used to this situation. But this was coming from our alley and there were only two house there - ours and Saeid's house. The thought of this made me nervous.

I said to my mother, "what's happening? God! Are they hurt?"

After the noise had abated, mother went for information. When she returned there were tears coursing down her cheeks. I ran to her, begging her to tell me what had happened? Unfortunately, the Taliban had beat Saeid and his father, and they had taken Leyla.

My legs turned to jelly when I heard this news. I leaned towards the clay wall and sank down on the ground. Anxiety was making me crazy. I said I should go.

Mother brushed the dust from the wall off my hair and said, "well, when you are feeling better, we'll go together".

We went to Saeid's home together. His mother was sitting in a corner, hunched over and so still, like a dead body. The poor woman was in shock. Saeid was propped up against the wall, his face all bloody. Mother went to Faezeh, and I went to Lina.

Faezeh told us that recently the Taliban had become suspicious of so much movement in the area and they had investigated some of the students in the street. And that is how they finally found out about the school in this house. One day two of the Taliban came and ordered them to shut down the school. Saeid's family talked it over and consulted with the residents from the next alley. We promised to cancel the school, but Leyla had a strong will, and she continued her teaching without her father's knowledge. She told the students that they must be more careful - she recommended that they hide their books and notebooks under the Quran. If they were asked by the Taliban about them, they were to say they were learning from the holy book of Islam, the Quran.

When Saeid's father heard about it he yelled angrily, "you damn woman! Why are you only telling us about such an important issue now?".

Faezeh wiped her tears away with a corner of her hijab and said that Leyla had asked her not to tell anyone. She didn't want them to be worried.

Saeid said, "what's done is done. Let's hope that Leyla's work doesn't cost her, her head. He stood up then and said, "I should go to the law office and look for her".

I said, "but first we should tend to your wounds".

I took some cotton and alcohol from Lina and treated Saeid's wounds gently. His sad face reflected untold misery. He knew Leyla would never return.

He pulled himself together, thanked me and then said, "I will go".I

was worried sick. I said without thinking, "can't you leave it?".

Mother bit her lips and looked at me meaningfully, but his father agreed with me and said, "it is better if I go. You are young and headstrong. You may fight again. I will go. I may be able to achieve something if I beg and implore". The poor old man struggled to get up, took his hat, and his walking stick and set off.

Saeid said, "it is impossible to stay in this country, I wish Leyla could be released. If she is, we'll not stay here for one more day".

His mother agreed.

I was very worried. I said to myself 'what about me, where is my place in Saeid's destiny?' My mother become aware of my worry and whispered to me "if they do leave, we will go, too."

Saeid followed us to the door, I managed to ask him calmly, "you are really leaving? What about me?"

He smiled gently and said, "you are my breath, wherever I go, no matter how difficult, I will take you with me".

I said, "but how? Maybe Hadji Rasoul's long absence has made you brave".

Saeid replied, "if I am not brave, I will take my dreams to the grave".

I was searching for an answer to Saeid, when mother helped me.

She said "let's go…, goodbye, goodbye".

It was another day in autumn when someone knocked loudly on our door. Anxiety surged through every inch of my body.

I yelled at Parvin, my little sister, "go, don't you hear?"

She went to see who it was and came back very distressed and said, "Lina has come; it looks like she brings bad news".

Lina was breathing fast I forgot to even say hello.

I asked, "what happened?".

She was almost in a state of collapse but managed to say, "morning… morning. I've come to tell you we will be burying Leyla".

I said, "what are you talking about?"

She cried, and said, "today we were told that the judge's order had been done and that we can come and take away the body. My father and Saeid have gone. I should go back now; my mother is alone."

My mother and I accompanied Lina back to their house to offer our sympathy to Faezeh. Seeing the situation that Saeid's family were in made me very unhappy. Soon, Saeid and his father returned.

I turned to Saeid and said, "the punishment for running a school for girls in your house is not meant to be death".

He said, "it has its story".

I stared into his eyes curiously. A tear drop appeared on his cheek, as he tried not to show his hatred. The judge in Leyla's case proposed to Leyla and said if you marry me, you will be free, otherwise, the crime of adultery will be added to your case! Her bravery is what killed Leyla.

Saeid's father said through his tears, "my little girl always said, women have the right to choose. She finally chose death over coercion." After his words, he lost self-control, and his weak shoulders started shaking. I could do nothing but watch such huge amounts of sorrow at these unfortunate events.

The funeral was over. Saeid's family was tired of everything and everyone and turned into sad corpses. Faezeh stared into the corner of the wall for hours and sometimes called us Leyla, by mistake. When she remembered that they had killed her daughter for something legal and accepted all over the world, she cried hysterically. It was like Saeid's father had had his back broken in this situation, but he always said, 'I have no guilty feeling toward my conscience, I lost my child in the path of knowledge and science'. Good for Leyla who died with a good reputation and the respect of others. She always believed that women should be able to study and progress? And she finally lost her life following this path".

***

The cold season of winter had begun. Hadji and his sons hung around the house in the warm and forgot about their work. Meanwhile, the work for my mother and me become more arduous. In the severe cold without facilities, we were struggling to manage. I don't know where the honor was in the prejudice of Zaher, my half-brother, at that time? He hurt me often, and was often trying to get close to me wherever and whatever I was doing. I would happily have sliced off his hands like a fish, to escape his attentions and preserve my decency.

He didn't see me as a sister, and one day he pushed me into a corner of the kitchen forcing me up against the wall and put his hand on my breasts, saying "you are so adorable, I won't lose you, I will talk to father to propose to you for me".

I said, "be ashamed, I am your sister".

He laughed loudly and said, "which sister? Neither our father nor mother are the same. So, we can marry each other."

I couldn't talk and said "I ... I hate you". He slapped me hard and laughed and moved away and said, "we will see... you are mine".

Three months of winter were always a nightmare for me, since the men were in our home. I thought, what if Hadji agrees and gives me to Zaher? If this happens, I will kill myself. I wanted Saeid and only thought of him, and no one else.

I wanted to tell my mother about what Zaher had said, but it was certain that mother would then talk to Hadji, and he would probably soonengage me to Zaher to prevent us from sin, so I hid the secret in my deep conscience. I didn't see Saeid for three months and I became desperate. Not even a few minutes meeting. At nights, I wrote down all my bitter and sweet memories, and complained about Saeid's remoteness. My pure love turned me into an unknown author.

At night, I thought it was the last minutes before the end of the world. Every instance of impolite behavior and unnecessary words was like a sting to my heart. Destiny made wounds on my heart, so I neglectedany kind of cure and treatment. I had passed the desert of my destiny, with all its ups and downs until now. Whenever thirst annoyed me, I asked for some water from travelers, and they directed me to the sea. I took the address but fell and stood again with dried lips. When I got to my destination, because of my bad fortune, the sea was empty and its fishes were dead. The smell of their corpses caused me to suffer, too. I continued this journey very thirsty and tired, with the hope of a merciful rain over my dry destiny. Saeid was the only reason for my living. He was the only bridge between death and life. If he wasn't here, life and rehabilitation would die for me. The moment of being with him was the time of rebirth.

The winter of that night passed like a century to me. My heart was like a fireplace that couldn't be extinguished with any water. The memory of Saeid made waves in the sea of my heart. But nobody knew about my situation. Nobody knew what damage separation had on me. My mother was drowning in her own troubles, she couldn't see my suffering. Whenever I found something that Saeid had written, I read it many times. I memorized every word of it. I missed him so much, but unfortunately, I didn't know to give myself to what breeze, to get to my lover. The morning breeze had the smile of his happy laughs and recalled the warmth of his manly hands. In the afternoon, the poems he had read to me came to mind. The evening wind touched my face while he wrote, or while he toyed with my hair. It smelled like the nights of isolation when I talked with him, while I was laying with a burned body on the hospital bed. I talked of pain, and he showed me how to heal. When my eyes locked onto his, the decency of the girl within me, modestly moved my eyes in another direction.

After three months, I knew I was in love, and our separation would be like a death. Inevitably I became ready to fight, to remove the obstacles from the path of our happiness. Happiness. It had no other meaning for me other than the warm embrace of my lover. Yes, all the cells of my body called for him. I wanted him, because he was such a comfort to me. Since he was a free person, he had taught me to be a free human being, too.

Finally, the cold and soulless winter of that year finished and the beautiful spring scattered flowers on the tired land. Saeid's family still wore the black clothing as a sign for mourning, because of Leyla's death. My mother selected one of the days of Nowruz[5] to remove the clothes of sadness from them. After Hadji's working travels recommenced, my mother and I went to Saeid's house.

His father opened the door for us; the poor old man was totally broken, like he had been sick for many years.

He said, "please come in, my sister, …, welcome".

Mother said, "thank you, Hadji Saheb". She continued, "you are still wearing black, please remove these clothes".

The old man didn't respond to my mother but turned and called loudly, "Lina, we have guests. Please come in, come in". Lina came to us and after greeting us, she guided us in.

We sat on the pad on one side of the room. The soul of happiness was gone from their house. Everyone was sad.

Dear Faezeh said, "well, you finally came".

My mother said, "don't make us feel guilty; you know our situation. For these last few months, the men were home, and we couldn't come out, but we were always thinking of you".

Lina said, "we do understand and don't complain; everyone has their own problems".

While Lina was talking, Saeid entered the room and said 'hello'.

My mother and I stood up as custom and good manners dictated. He said, "please, you are very welcome".

When I looked at Saeid he was so attractive, he made my heartbeat many times faster.

Lina, who sat behind me, detected it and said in my ear, "what is it? Why are you stressed?"

I couldn't talk about it, so I said, "nothing, nothing happened".

---

[5] Nowruz is a festival in March celebrating the New Year Based on the Persian calendar.

Lina smiled a little and said, "be calm".

I couldn't hear what anyone was saying. I only had two eyes to watch the kind looks of my lover. Maybe I wanted to deliver my unspoken words to him through my eyes. But how? How could I say, 'my comfort space, understand my feelings'? If you don't understand it, it will turn into ash in the fire of your isolation. See how easy you imprisoned me, an unbreakable link which is available only through your achievement".

The voice of dear Faezeh, brought me to my senses. I turned my eyes away from Saeid, and looked at his mother and said, "yes".

Mother said, "they called you many times".

I said with shame, "excuse me".

Faezeh said, "I wanted to know, how do you spend your days?"

I replied, "dear aunt, no woman believes in herself to do anything; I do almost nothing but cooking and cleaning. But sometimes I study."

Saeid used the opportunity to ask me, "how was the book I sent you last week?"

I said, "thank you, it was very good. All the history of Afghanistan was written in it; it was very useful, and I shall read it again".

He said, if conditions were different, you would be an educated girl".

I said, "my bad luck started when I lost my father. As mother said, he was an open-minded person and valued freedom".

Saeid's father said, "God bless him,"

Then my mother answered "God bless your dead too. Roya's father was killed by these extremist Muslims. Anyway, I came here to ask you to remove your black clothes. Even Leyla would not be happy with this prolonged mourning."

Then she got up and went to Faezeh and removed the black scarf and replaced it with a new white scarf she had brought with her. She gave a white shirt to Hadji Zabih.

She said, "you change your clothes, too. It is the new year, it's time for you to come out of this mourning".

Hadji said, "God bless you our sister, thank you for thinking about us".

Then mother said, "well, if you let us, we will go now".

Saeid's mother and sister accompanied us, Parvin and Pouran were playing with Saeid. He liked children very much.

He came close when he saw us, and said, "are you leaving?"

I said, "if you permit". He gave me a special look and said, "if it was up to me, I'd never let you go".

I smiled and bowed my head. My mother and lady Faezeh understood Saeid's words and walked away to give us some privacy.

It was just me and my lover. He took my hand gently and came closer. The scent of him touched my face like a cool and slow breath. Without realizing what I was doing, I saw my hands on Saeid's shoulders. When my mother and Faezeh came back, I lost myself completely, but my mother didn't care and said, "time to go". I still couldn't stop looking at Saeid and didn't want to leave. so, I answered, "I will come when I've said goodbye".

Then I whispered in Saeid's ear, "leaving you is like dying but there is no other way. If you don't have anything else to say, I will go".

He said with his customary humor, "I do have things to say to you, but you don't give me time".

He then handed me a letter and said, "I wrote all my ideas in this. Write and think about them comprehensively".

I pressed his hand warmly and said goodbye.

At night, when I was going to bed, I opened the letter. The beautiful and calm face of Saeid was summoned in my mind. It was like I was in his warm embrace, and listening to his sweet words.

'A warm hello like the hot love in my body; you know that at this moment I need a kind friend like you by my side more than anything. And you need someone like me as a support. Since I saved you from the flames, I have put myself in an oven from which there is no escape except when I am with you. Sweetheart, I want to say something to you - I won't hide anything from you. If you want to be my partner in this hard life, and insist on marrying me, make yourself ready. By the end of the third month, my family and I will migrate to Iran. I would be glad to have the warmth of your hands, on this difficult journey. Think about it and talk to your mother, so that in the future, we will become a good couple. Despite all our troubles we can lead a good life together. If you want to talk about it with me and my family, I shall be waiting here for you, your lover, Saeid".

When my mother came to bed, I told her about Saeid's letter. Her eyes become full of tears and a deep hatred prevented her from speaking.

I said, "if you don't agree, I won't go. Please don't be upset; I can't bear to see your tears".

She said, "but you should go with Saeid; he is your dream man. I don't want to deprive you of this opportunity. I wouldn't like to be sorry in front of your dead father. In the morning we will go to Saeid's house to speak more about this. Maybe there is a better way." And she turned her sad and frustrated face away, so that I wouldn't see the sorrow of separation from her child in her eyes. She said, "sleep my daughter, we will talk about it in the morning".

Yes, she wanted to drown alone in sadness, in the comfort of her bed. Very simply, her wishes faded away in the cloudy sky of life, like a bubble that had burst. And now she was afraid that I would become a puppet in the hand of others, for them to toy with as they pleased. Maybe she was thinking about how she could save her daughter from such a destiny.

Whatever she thought about, it was very sad for her, and from time to time, a painful sigh escaped her lips. This painful music to my ears, invited me in to her sad mind. Yes, I thought of her; in the spring of her youth her life became a disaster as a result of my father's death. The reality was that poverty forced her to leave the life she knew and to go to people with vastly different ideas. Now for me, she had to accept another form of coercion. So, when would she ever get to live in the way that her heart desired?

These thoughts were on my mind like annoying flies, buzzing around, making my conscience uncomfortable. I said to myself. 'I shouldn't add another sadness to her pains, no way should I enforce another pressure on her'.

That night was one of the longest nights in a long time. All sorts of annoying ideas went through my head. Finally, when dawn came, my eyes became heavy and I slept.

***

I was telling stories to Pouran and Parvin in one corner of the room. They stared at me with their black eyes and heavily fringed with eyelashes. As I paused for a moment, they couldn't wait to hear the rest of the story; they said together with curiosity, "well, … what next?"

And as I continued with excitement in my voice, my mother called me and said, "after the end of the story come to kitchen, I have work for you".

I acknowledged her words by nodding my head. I finished the story quickly, and went to kitchen to my mother, who was cooking the lunch.

I sat beside her on a chair, and said, "what work do you have for me, dear mother?"

She said, "I wanted to talk about you and Saeid. Today I will go to their house and talk to his mother and father. Let's see what their plan is. If we agree, you and Saeid can talk in the morning too. Hadji won't be back from his travels yet. You can get to know each other better and then God be with you,"

When she said her last sentence, my eyes were full of tears. She walked away in order to look at the food she was cooking, so I wouldn't see her tears. She wanted to endure her sadness alone.

I stood up and went to her and said, "dear mother, do you agree from the bottom of your heart?"

She said, "life has never gone according to my wishes until now, so why should this be any different?"

I said, "this time you can say anything you want".

Well, I say you and Saeid get married, have a huge wedding, so I can say I sent my daughter to destiny's house with respect and dignity. I will have grandchildren; you will become a teacher and go to your work duties. Me and Faezeh will keep our grand-children …".

These were her wishes. When she had finished, she asked, "is it possible?".

Well, these were the simple wishes and demands of any woman, but they were unavailable for me and her. Inevitably and with shame I said, "you know it is impossible".

She said, "now you believe that we can't live according to our wishes? We should accept the destiny because of one wish, and other wishes should be forgotten. Now for your happiness and future, I will be deprived from seeing your beautiful face".

She couldn't hold back her hatred of our situation anymore, and hugged me unconsciously. We both cried for this unfortunate life …, that we were doomed to live without ever getting what we wanted. Spit on this destiny, … spit on injustice.

The initial talks were held about my wedding with Saeid. Everything was agreed. On one spring day of that year we were engaged in secret, hidden and only acknowledged in the presence of my mother and Saeid's mother. Our destinies were linked together irrevocably.

With all my happiness, I still could feel a strange sadness deep inside me. Everyone who was present came close and congratulated me. But I was drowned in my own thoughts. ... what ceremony? I had no father to support me. My mother stood lonely in one corner and watched the isolation of her child.

The memory of that day was bitter-sweet to me. I acquired the love of Saeid, but I wouldn't be able to experience the warm embrace of a devoted mother anymore. That day I talked with Saeid, and it was agreed that I wouldn't see him again until we were due to set off on our journey. I wanted to be as long as possible with my mother and enjoy her warm presence while I still could.

Those days I never lost sight of my mother. Something told me that after this separation, I would never see her again. I didn't know where these events would take me. The fearful nightmare of our future stole the sleep from my eyes. At nights, I went near my mother's bed and looked at her tired face for hours. How could I leave her alone with the shame and blame she would endure from others? No, God I couldn't do it. Why? Why should I have to experience this destiny?

Separation was like a dark shadow over my future. Every day that passed, the light became weaker. Gradually, we got close to the promised day. My mother and I became more and more anxious. She was anxious about my migration and I about her situation without me.

It was the end of September. According to the arrangements, my mother and I would meet Saeid's family at the cemetery. That is where I would join them to travel to Iran. I was unlucky because that particular time Taher hadn't travelled with Hadji. Anxiety covered all of my body. I didn't know what was mother's plan to allow me to escape. At night, I went over to her bed. She woke up gently and sat up. I rested my head on her knees.

She touched my hair and said, "tomorrow morning is the time to leave. Are you ready?"

I said, "for leaving with Saeid yes, but for separation from you, never!".

She said, "my little girl, you should be strong. Do what you have learned until today in your life, all except one thing - silence against injustice. The venom called silence destroys the human soul piece by piece. Don't let others decide for you. If I had stood against the demands of my father, I wouldn't have to be separated from my dear child".

As she said these words, my hair was soaked from her tears. I stood up and hugged her.

Until midnight, mother and I were together; she talked and I listened. She taught me everything a girl should learn. She told about what would happen on my wedding night, and about being a mother. She answered my questions so that she didn't send her girl unprepared to her destiny.

I asked, "what is your plan for tomorrow?" She said that she had asked Taher to take us to Shahzadeha (a cemetery in Herat).

Surprised, I said, "we go with Taher? That way we will all die".

She said, "is it not true that in this country women can only go outside when accompanied by their men?"

I said, "true".

Mother said, "so don't interfere, and do as I say".

That night I slept on her warm knee, the very last time I would have her support.

It was Thursday. With a lot of worry, we went to the cemetery - my mother, two small sisters and Taher - to the tombs. Everyone sat and read the Quran.

My mother took the pitcher, and said, "my girl, Roya, go and bring water to wash your father's tomb".

I understood my mother's plan but hesitated. She told me to go again, very emphatically. My eyes were like plates of blood. I wanted to yell. Hatred blocked my throat. I hugged Pouran and Parvin unconsciously and kissed them fiercely.

Mother didn't want to let Taher become suspicious of my behaviour so she yelled, "I'm not going to tell you again? Go and bring the water now".

I took the pitcher and moved toward the well. In the distance, I saw Saeid standing there.

He came forward and said, "why are you late?".

I said, "I can't come with you anywhere; they will hurt my mother".

He said, "we talked before. Should I go my love? I told your mother to say she doesn't know anything about us when we left".

Then he took my hand and continued, "be calm, afraid of nothing. I won't leave you alone, come… come before Taher follows you".

I escaped with Saeid. But my heart was with my mother, hidden behind her hijab.

As I got further away from there, I felt closer to Saeid. When we got to the road, I saw Saeid's family waiting for us near a carrier vehicle. Quickly and quietly, we climbed inside the vehicle. And kept moving. Everyone, except me, had one small pack for the journey. I was lighter and sadder than anyone else.

Saeid's mother hugged me and said, "welcome to our family".

I just cried and didn't have a response.

Hadji Zabih turned to me and said, "from now on, I am your father and Faezeh is your mother and Lina your sister; don't think about anything else. You are going to start a new life. Meanwhile, for the duration of our journey, if anyone asks you, tell them you are Saeid's wife. You and Lina should represent yourself as weak women. Don't show your face to any man; many girls have been stolen."

When Saeid's father had finished speaking, I slipped into my dark isolation again. As the vehicle drove on, it felt like my heart had detached from my chest and was being trampled into the ditch by the side of the road. The red flowers on my scarf were drowned in my tears. My black hijab didn't allow anyone to see the drowning of the flowers, unable to offer any help. Gradually, the source of my tears dried up. I closed my eyes and listened to the prayers of Saeid's mother. Whispering the prayers Faezeh was reciting made me calm again. I leaned toward the almighty supernatural power, so that I could tolerate the desperation and separation.

I was sunk deep in the sea of my thoughts when the vehicle stopped. The sadness in my heart was instantly replaced with fear.

Saeid noticed my fright and said, "don't worry, it's just a simple check point. Everyone get out of the vehicle and remain calm".

Hadji Zabih and the driver got out of the front of vehicle. The driver was a big man, with a long beard, and a crazy old hat on his head. Although in those days, all men were similar to each other and all looked angry.

Three armed Talibs with a child were on the road. Everyone got down from the vehicle.

One of the Talibs directed Saeid towards the place where his father stood and when he had joined him he asked Hadji violently, "where are you going?"

"Islam Qala[6], to my brother's house. My nephew has died and we are in mourning".

"Well, what relationship are these other people to you?"

---

[6] Islam Qala is the name of a town in Kahsan district in the western part of Herat province, Afghanistan, located at the zero point of the Afghan border with the city of Taybad in Iran.

"They are my family"

When one of them pointed, the child with them came to us. My body was totally shaking. God, what are they going to do? When the boy get closer, my heart beat faster. He came close and raised up my hijab, his innocent and dusty face, showed his tired character. I said to myself, "they are definitely taking advantage of this child. He should be in the school like his friends, not doing this here in their service".

"Who are you looking for? Let's go," I heard Lina say.

"Where?"

"Eslam Ghale Didn't you hear?"

They let us go.

Everyone got back in the vehicle again. When my hand was on Saeid's warm hand, I felt much better. His presence was a hope and support to me.

I asked Saeid, "why did that boy investigate under the women's hijabs?"

He said, "so the men who are being perused and are trying to escape, don't disguise themselves in women's clothes". I

I said, "Saeid, what do you think my mother is doing now?"

"I don't know."

"I know, she will be punished for what I have done."

"You aren't supposed to be thinking about it anymore. What is done is done and nothing can change that now. At least don't make life bitter for yourself and us. She is a wise woman; she definitely had a plan to take care of the situation."

While we were speaking, his mother brought us a piece of tasty homemade bread with some thick yoghurt, from out of her pack and gave them to us. Saeid broke the bread into pieces and fed me, with love. It was a scene that very few women in Afghanistan will have experienced. There was a huge distance between men and women in our city. If somebody did what Saeid was doing now, his masculinity would be in doubt. But despite his family living in the same environment, they had different ideas. It had been the unlimited kindness of Saeid that had attracted me to him.

I don't know for how many hours we travelled, but after a period, the vehicle stopped next to a big wooden door.

Saeid said, "I think we are guests in this house for tonight".

Everyone got down, and the driver knocked on the door. After a moment, a tall and middle-aged man opened the door to us. We entered a long, dark corridor, which branched off into two, leading to the men and women's houses, separate from each other. My eyes followed Saeid's footsteps. I was upset at being separated from him, but I had to go to the women's house with Lina and his mother. A woman dressed in a colourful and flowing robe came to us and accompanied us.

It was a quite a big hall with curtains, red-pile carpets and pillows. Two middle-aged women and their three daughters were in the place and welcomed us. Some other families like us were also guests of this house. An old woman on the other side of the hall sat in front of us. Maybe she was the doyen of the family. But seeing her angry eyebrows reminded me of Azim's mother who wanted to take me to her son's house. I was shaken by this thought, and unconsciously I leaned on the shoulder of Saeid's mother.

As I understood it, those two middle-aged women belonged to the house owner's household. The old lady was his mother who sat on the chair of power. I felt that old woman would take revenge on her son's brides for the previous cruelties inflicted on her when she herself first came into this household, and so it is that this cycle still goes on.

We slept that night in the house. It was the first night of sleeping without my mother. The hand of Saeid's mother was on my hand until morning, but how could I compare the soft and tiny hands of lady Faezeh, with tired and bony hands of my mother? Remembering the warmth of those tired hands made me relax. But the memory of her sad look made me frustrated with the world and its people. It was midnight when my eyelids finally closed and I sank into a warm and welcoming sleep.

In the morning when I woke up, I saw before me somewhere other than the cold room of my childhood. I remembered I had escaped from that damned place and left my mother beyond a separation of flames through which I could never return. Hadji wasn't there to curse me because I was late with his breakfast and my mother wasn't there to ask for patience with his tired look. Well, instead of all these things – both good and bad - I had the kind shadow of Saeid with me.

The voice of Faezeh, interrupted my thoughts as she called, "girls wake up, it is morning". Lina and I got up quickly, we arranged our beds and put the things on the side.

Lina asked, "did you sleep well last night?"

"No. Until midnight I was thinking about my mother. She definitely will have had a bad night, but her real troubles will start when Hadji returns from his travels."

Faezeh said, "you should practice forgetting, otherwise you will have a bitter life".

We saw the owner of the house later. According to Afghan hospitality this family was very kind to us, and they served us well. Although we didn't understand what they said because they spoke a special dialect, the dark eyes of the daughter held a special kindness.

The hard working women of that house, reminded me of my mother. Terror was evident in the houses along the border of Afghanistan at that time. Everybody had some kind of fear and stress. When there was a knock on the door they would hide us somewhere. The men of that house smuggled migrants across the border and if the Taliban knew, it was not known what horrible sentence they would issue for them.

We stayed in that house until the afternoon, and we ate delicious chorba with home-made bread. After the evening prayer, we kept moving towards the Iranian border along with other families from different cities. Two guides moved in front of us and we and rest of people moved in a line like worker ants.

I approached Saeid and asked, "for how long should we walk?"

He had a bitter smile and said, "I think until sunrise".

It seemed mandatory and I gathered all my force and continued to walk. The mountains and valleys which would have been enjoyable at any other time now seemed terrifying for me that night. Me, a girl who had never left her home before, was now alone and without my family in deserts and mountains, heading towards some unknown land?

Everyone kept going, through hills and valleys. Saeid's father said he couldn't walk anymore. He sat down after a few steps, but inevitably stood up again. Saeid took hold of him under his arm and helped him along. Lina and I were taking care of his mother. Our feet were burning and it showed that we had gone a long way.

Everyone was sunk in their own difficulties when Lina suddenly said loudly, "do you hear that?"

Everyone listened and said, "it is the sound of water".

Gradually under the light of moon, the width of the river became clear.

The guides turned to us and said, "you must help each other; we have to cross this water".

His words took us by surprise. If the waves should take us in the darkness of night, what would we do?

Hadji Zabih said, "you! Man! You took a lot of money from us to take us to a destination with these difficulties?"

The man knew we had no one else to help us; he laughed loudly and said "you expected to fly in an aeroplane? Anyone who wants to can cross the water with us, otherwise you can go back. Make up your minds but be quick; if daylight comes before we cross, we are all stuck. We must pass the border before the dawn".

Saeid calmed his father and said, "I will go first to discover the depth of the water. The rest of you come after me in pairs - young people help the older ones and the children".

The level of water reached to just under Saeid's chest. When he went, others became brave enough to follow him, too. Those who had children with them sat them on their shoulders while others took the hands of the older people. I was shaking, because the water was very cold.

When we got to the middle of the river, the water was up to our shoulders. The flow of water pulled at our veils. The force of the fast flowing water pulled at our feet, too, and there was a very real danger that we would be swept away and lost forever. It was unclear what path to take through the flow of water. We all made it to the far side and with the severe desert wind pulling at our sodden clothes, we continued on our weary footsore way.

A little girl, whose shoe was lost in the water, cried a lot. "Mother, I want to sleep - for the sake of God, can I sleep here?".

Her mother didn't have any power to hug her child; she took her hand and carried on. She was afraid that her child would become isolated and lost in the middle of nowhere. Sometimes she hugged the girl and when her energy was gone, she put her on the ground again, and the little girl continued to cry.

Everybody was desperate and frustrated. Everyone was just trying to take care of themselves. Only when we occasionally came face to face with each other did we sometimes think to ask about the others. It was like resurrection day; all of us were moving to an unknown destination, very tired and completely desperate.

We passed canebrakes and deserts, and finally reached the roadside. When the guides stopped, we all fell to the ground like corpses, all over the place. After a short rest, two Toyota motors appeared on the road.

Everyone was frightened that maybe the difficulty of coming up to here had all been wasted.

I approached Saeid and said, "who are these people?" He said, "stay calm, they won't bother us".

At the same time I heard the vehicles braking, I heard one of guides say, "don't be afraid, they are known to us".

The drivers got out of vehicles and spoke to our guides in Persian.

Saeid said, "I think we are to travel the rest of the journey in these two vehicles".

And his guess was right. From now on, these two people would be taking responsibility for us all.

Everybody was very tired, and were grateful to be sitting in the vehicles as they sped along the road. I was too frustrated to sleep. After a short ride, we stopped by the door of a house that belonged to one of the drivers. He led us into the house with great anxiety and care, and repeatedly advised us not to make any noise or leave the house in case the neighbours might see us. The women changed their normal hijabs for prayer clothes. The men put on the traditional clothes of Iran.

Now, I was many miles away from my mother. I looked at the desperate faces of my accompanies, and began to cry. Nobody knew when or where this trip would end? The dust and tiredness of travel, made everyone's face look frustrated and angry. It was like everyone was returning home from a long war. They greedily ate the yoghurt and bread of the home owner as if they had just escaped from a famine. What can be said about the pain of homeless people?

This was just the beginning of our long journey. We all changed our clothes and were ready to move on. Saeid shaved his face and put on a formal suit. I thought he looked very appealing and handsome. I was honoured with my choice, in my heart.

Lina understood my looks and smiled and said, "Is he good looking?"

I said, "who?"

She said, "you know who I mean. Don't tease".

And we both laughed loudly.

Her mother said, "your tiredness has gone and you are ready to start again?".

We were in the middle of talking, when they informed us it was time to go. We went outside one by one and entered the vehicle. We had now passed the danger point. Everyone was hopeful and smiling. I didn't know for how many hours we drove for, but this period passed very quickly. Gradually, the holy pillars of the mosque appeared in Mashhad's skyline. Everyone felt great joy, combined with a huge sadness. Yes, everyone had escaped the war, and were now confined to desperation and exile.

We had entered an unknown country. All of us looked around with anxiety. Hadji Zabih searched his pocket as soon as he got out of vehicle.

He went toward a telephone kiosk and returned to us after a few minutes and said, "my friend will soon come to accompany us".

Our comrades said goodbye, one by one and each went in a different direction. We sat on the steps of a hotel very tired and desperate. Citizens searched out our identity with their looks, and they whispered to each other.

We were getting a little uncomfortable when Saeid finally got up and said, "father, Kaka has come".

Everyone turned to look. A man of medium height, and with a very clean and decent face came up to us. After searching, we took a taxi, and moved toward the house of Hadji Zabih's friend. Kaka Rahim's house was built based on traditional Herat architecture. It was clean and organized and as Heratis say, "if you dropped oil, it is easily gathered". Kaka's wife was kind and beautiful.

After a heartfelt greeting, she turned to her aunt, Faezeh, and said "sister, what a beautiful bride you have brought with you".

Faezeh proudly said, "they just got engaged, and the wedding arrangements require your help. We have no one except you". Kaka's wife responded kindly, "we are all desperate, I don't know the curse of which demon was sent to the people of Afghanistan to create such misery. We should help each other in this foreign country. Saeid is like my own child, I won't withhold any help".

Lina entered the conversation and said "how is the situation here for Afghans?"

Kaka's wife said, "not very good. Whenever their pockets are empty, they claim they are hiring Afghans, and after taking a huge fund from international organizations, they shut down. Last year, they cruelly loaded many families equipment on trucks and sent them back over the border".

On hearing the words of kaka's wife, I knew that although we might share the same religion and language with these people, we were nothing more than strangers in this city. I should prepare myself for harsh words and bad feelings. We are neighbours but we aren't relaxed with each other. I shouted at myself "you poor girl! You escaped from where to where? You left your own country to search for what in this country?"

With the help and guidance of Kaka Rahim, we rented a house, and followed the required process to get our identity cards.

Chapter 6

The sound of raindrops hitting the glass, attracted my attention toward the old, wooden window of the room. Summer turned the garden into a new place, beautiful and adorable. I opened the window and looked out to see the clear raindrops sitting inside a red flower. The smell of straw filled the space, and there was no sound other than the rain. It seemed that like me, everybody was enjoying the peace and quiet. I was surrounded by my thoughts, when two manly arms hugged me in an embrace and a voice whispered in my ear, "you are enjoying the rain alone again?"

He raised me up above him and sat down on the edge of the bed that was piled in the corner of the room. Our eyes met.

Saeid said, "now tell me what you were thinking?"

I said slowly, "first, you put me down, and then I will tell you".

He swung me back down so that my feet were back on the ground and I sat down beside him.

"Well,… I am waiting," he said.

"I was thinking about the future," I replied.

"Promise me you will always think about the future and forget the past. Also I have some good news."

"News! From where? Afghanistan?"

"You promised a few minutes ago. Forget it?"

"Now, tell me the news."

"You and Lina can study at nights."

"I … can study?"

"If you like, but firstly you must do a test."

I became very happy, hugged him and he laughed saying, "from now on, I will bring you good news everyday".

I knew what he meant and released him in my embarrassment and said, "did you find a job?"

But Saeid didn't answer my question.

When Lina entered and said, "father called you," we went to the livingroom together and sat.

Father started talking and said, "well, dear Saeid, what did you do today? Did you find a job?"

"No, everywhere they say do you have a work permit?, A university degree is useless. Educated Iranian guys are unemployed, so what hope is there for us? I had to work with Samei finally."

"What is his job?"

Scaffolding. It is a hard and dangerous job. After two months of searching, I know now that the only work available to Afghans is hard and dangerous, without insurance and with a low salary. That's if they are aren't spotted by the work ministry staff, otherwise they are sent to the camp.

Mother groaned and said, "damn them, we will end up homeless. My son shouldn't have to do this after all those years of studying".

Saeid said, "don't be sad mother, these days will end, and hard work is a man's lot. We must put our hope in God, and from tomorrow morning I work with Samei. Father, if you will allow it, I will send Lina and Roya to school."

Father and Faezeh said together, "it is very well".

Father started talking again, "OK, you three have a clear situation, and your mother will work at home. I will work at the draper's shop. Thank God, everybody will be doing something from tomorrow, so life won't be too hard. Anybody listening to his conscious as a behavioural guide won't be ashamed."

Mother said, "what about Saeid and Roya's wedding; it is not right to be engaged for such a long time".

Father answered, "wait until we are settled here, then we will consider that, too. And I cannot accept the groom until he has an income."

For one second I thought it was my father who was defending his own daughter.

Mother surrendered to her husband's logical decision and said, "now girls, bring the tea".

Living with Saeid and his family was unlike anything I had ever experienced before. Everybody knew his or her duty, and nothing was forced on anyone.

With Saeid's help Lina and I did our test. We registered for the eleventh grade. We would go to school starting from the autumn. I was very interested in studying. Learning and knowledge shed light on the dark stories. Freedom was a weird but sweet feeling for me. Saeid was my only concern, he wasn't adapting well to his new environment. He was disappointed and that was right. After all his years of studying, he had now become a simple manual worker, which he found humiliating. But he did not voice any word of complaint against his situation. If I asked, he would answer shortly, "thank God" and excuse himself. Maybe he just didn't want to bother me with complaints. Half of his salary was spent on household expenses and the other half was used for purchasing new furniture for our house.

***

During that time we were like two lovebirds; together we gathered things to make a house on a tree of kindness where we would raise our chick in its warmth. Life had new meaning for me. My legs had the power to take a run at the turns along life's long road. Sometimes slow, sometimes fast and sometimes creeping. But always moving forward. Spring, summer, autumn, winter passed with desperation and beauty. Autumn recalled the sad face of my own mother. Winter was like her cold fingers. Memories of the past, balanced the beam of life; the dark clown of my destiny mocked me with a laugh. The days and months dragged slowly on as one season after another passed by.

***

One year had passed since I took leave of the old, cold house of my childhood and moved to this small but warm house with Saeid and his family. Norouz Day was here again, and Lina and I were cooking in the kitchen and laughing together when we heard father come home.

"Where are you Roya?"

We went out to the garden to welcome him. He always returned home with full hands.

I said, " hello, dear father".

He said, "hello to you, my beautiful bride".

I took the fruit and cookies he had brought for us and thanked him.

I was going to go back to the kitchen when he said, "don't you want to ask what these cookies are for?"

I said, " what are they for?"

He said replied, "no, you must guess".

I begged, "I can't guess. Please tell me!"

He kissed my forehead, smiled and said, "I asked my friend who was travelling to Afghanistan if he would go to see your mother and tell her how you are, and to ask about her for you".

I said with excitement, "well?"

"Now my friend has returned and has told me that your mother is well."

He put his hand in his pocket and took out a ring and gave it to me. I recognised it as my mother's ring, which proved to me that she was still alive and in good health.

I became tearful and ran to my room. I put my head against the wall and cried for the past, forgetting the happiness that I had found with my new family. But the ring that had made my mother's hands beautiful was now a sacred sign. I kissed it many times as if it was my mother's hand, and promised to never let it go.

After a few minutes, Lina and Saeid came and said together, "you're crazy. You are crying instead of being happy?"

I lifted my head and told them it was nothing. After a while I became calmer. Lina sat beside me and took my hand.

She looked at the ring and said it was very beautiful.

I smiled gently and as I wiped my tears away I said, "it is the only souvenir from my father, but now mother has nothing to remember him by. A strange anger welled up inside my throat, and the tears started to flow once more. I couldn't stop the flood of my tears. Meanwhile, mother called us to come and eat.

Saeid looked at his sister and said, "you go and help your mother. I will come with Roya in a minute". Lina laughed and left us there alone.

Saeid hugged me and wiped away my tears. He said, "how long must I watch you crying? You cry both in sadness and in joy; now laugh".

I smiled and said, "well? Are you satisfied?"

He caressed me, teasingly. Our happy laughter filled the room until Lina called us mischievously to come and have dinner. We went together and sat at the table. Having received such news of my mother's good health, a mountain of concern was removed from my shoulders. I felt lighter. Now I could get on with my life without all that worry.

After we had finished eating and cleared the table, father said to us all, "are we finally ready to receive the bride into our home? You have bought everything for her?".

Saeid and mother said in chorus, "yes, sir".

Lina continued, "God bless all the daughters from such a father-in-law". I didn't say anything but just laughed.

Mother said, "this oppression affects us all. You, Lina, you shouldn't tease them like that, or you will end up in a pickle".

Father looked at me, without paying any attention to either his wife or daughter.

"It is good that you have such news from your mother. And now that your house is ready, you have no obstacles standing in the way of your happiness. Now go and bring the pastries and get ready to listen to some more good news."

I arranged the pastries on a tray and took them to my father-in-law. Everybody was listening carefully.

Saeid lost his patience and said, "what about this other good news".

Father said, "you have been in a hurry to become a groom. The next good news is you shall be married to Roya at last. When shall we eat your wedding feast?"

Saeid answered slowly with a smile on his lips, "whatever you and mother say, we will accept".

Mother said, "everything will be ready in two weeks".

Father added, "how about inviting our friends and relatives to come on Friday in two weeks' time? We'll provide a simple ceremony here in the garden, and then you two can go to your own house."

Everyone was very positive and full of joy to hear the news.

From the next day, work on preparing for the ceremony began. There was one big room and a small atrium on the other side of the garden. We painted them and arranged everything just how we wanted it. Faezeh made a blanket for the bed just like my own kind mother would have done. Mother talked to me about what would happen. I was only 17, but the difficulties and experiences I had already gone through had made me tough, and the typhoons of life were like a gentle breeze. I'd had a hard childhood and it had made my body hard like stone and my soul fragile like glass.

The wedding ceremony was done honorably and joyfully. We all congregated in our common house and promised never to leave each other alone. Nothing but death could separate us. That was the best day of my life. Saeid was glowing like a gem beside me. In my dreams I saw my mother who was looking at me proudly and adoringly. I raised my hand unconsciously to her.

Saeid noticed and said," are you daydreaming again, Roya?".

"It was nothing, I thought I saw my mother there in the crowd for one second."

"Beautiful lady, forget about crying for tonight."I said, "yes,
 dream's prince".

Saeid smiled and said, "it is our best night ever. Having you for my wife seemed like a distant dream on the far horizon, but now you are here with me".

I said, "yes, we made it, we passed the 'Seven Obstacles of Rostam[7]' and have this moment together. We should make the most of it as we'll never have this moment again."

He smiled, teasingly and said, "for sure. Especially when we are alone, you are indescribably beautiful tonight".

---

[7] Rostam was a legendary hero in Persian folklore immortalized by the tenth century poet, Ferdowsi, in the Shahnameh, or Epic of Kings, and Haft Khan Rostam are the names of the seven battles in Ferdowsi's Shahnameh that Rostam fought. Haft Khan Rostam is an allusion to the difficulty of what is to be done.

I said, jokingly, "you are a pervert really. No! I didn't mean that. You're all right."

He said, "I know".

Then Lina came and interrupted us, saying, "stop talking, you two. It's time to dance".

We were the happiest then than we had ever been or ever would be again.

It was past 2:00 am and Saeid's mother guided us towards our room. It was fresh and clean, like the sunrise, and a new life. It was unbelievable. Our dark fate had turned into a shining white angel, and we wished then that things would never change.

***

Slowly, the dark clouds were eliminated from our life, and the warm sunshine replaced them. I was very busy and didn't notice the time passing. I woke up happy in the mornings with Saeid's warm caresses. We'd get ready and then join Saeid's father and mother. We'd eat breakfast together with a smile, and then everyone would get on with their work.

Study and lessons were a joy to me, and Lina's teasing ways made it all the sweeter for me. We were in 12th grade and almost finished with school. Every afternoon after study, we would walk home past tiny, old alleys shrouded in darkness. Sometimes we would have to put up with the bothersome behavior of unemployed youths. When we got home mother would have tea ready for us.

After changing our clothes, we would go to the living room to have our tea. One day Lina and mother were talking.

I said "you are alone. Did you have company today?"

Mother smiled and said, "come, I have good news for you today".

I said, "I am listening".

She said, Samei's mother came with a proposal for Lina.

I smiled broadly and said, "Lina, it is your turn".

Lina said, "now what have you got to say?"

I said, "he is a good, hard-working guy. His family are good, too".

Mother said, "we should first consult with father and Saeid. Tonight, we will talk to them. Samei's mother will return for an answer tomorrow."

I said, "they will come before noon, so you should be here and ready for their return".

That night Saeid was very tired. I knew it wasn't only his body that was tired, but his soul was tired from life, too.

When he went to the garden to wash his hands, I followed him and sat beside the old fountain that was cracked from last winter's frost. He turned on the faucet and asked, "how was school, today?"

I told him about my day and then continued, "how was your job today?"

He told me that it had been fine, but I said that his face told me a different story.

He said, "I am just a little tired this evening".

I passed him the towel and said, "something is wrong, and you aren't telling me. I can see you are tired; it shows in your face".

He moved towards the door and said, "there's nothing for you to be concerned about".

When mother came, we stopped talking.

Mother asked me to come and help with the table, so I went with her.

After dinner, we talked about Samei's proposal.

Father said, "I've known this family from a long time ago. They are of honorable origin. But I don't know Samei. Saeid should tell us his opinion about this. Everyone looked at Saeid. He said with a serious face, "it is good. I know nothing bad about him. He is very patient."

I asked, "how do you know he is patient?"

"Because he has tolerated many difficulties in this area for many years."

Then I heard nothing else. I knew Saeid's job put him under a lot of mental pressure and he was very depressed. I was deep in my own thoughts when mother caught my attention. She put a dish of chocolate in front of me and said, "sweeten your mouth Roya".

I knew that Lina would be leaving this house soon. I was glad for her but knew I would miss her.

It was past 11 o'clock and we went to our room for the night. I set up the bed and went to brush my teeth. When I returned, Saeid was still awake.

I lay beside him, touched his black hair and said, "now you know the city better, can't you find a better job?".

He said, "what is your idea and why?"

I said, "don't play games with me anymore. I know you aren't satisfied."

Saeid told me, "The money isn't bad, and our life is good. It's working with them that is difficult. We are darned Afghans to them. Today one worker couldn't put up with the humiliation anymore and confronted the supervisor, and he was fired. I don't want to continue taking this sort of behavior from them".

I said, "so look for another job. With God's help, you might find a better job".

He just said, "don't think about it, just study. You have your final exam this year which is difficult enough without all this worry".

I kissed his lips and hugged him. The lack of his hug was certain death for me.

After that night I asked everyone, I knew, every friend and relative, about a job for Saeid, so I might release this pressure from my husband. The more I asked, the less I found. Saeid continued to do what he had to do – he had no other choice. Like the proverb, if the hand stops, the mouth stops. If he didn't work, we had nothing to eat.

***

That summer Lina and I took our exam and were successful in gaining our diploma. Those good days ended, and Lina's marriage ceremony went ahead without any problem. Then it was time for her to leave us to go to live in her new home. It was time for me to say goodbye to my dear kind friend and sister, Lina. It was a difficult day for me. My tears seemed endless. I couldn't bear it. Ours was not a happy household.

For the first month after Lina left, everyone was sad. I tried to be closer to mother so she wouldn't feel the isolation from her daughter so much. She accepted me with open arms. After school had finished, and Lina had left, nothing new happened for a long time. We all got on with our work. Empty days passed by, and the white pages of our memories become dark.

***

It was near the end of azar, or December, when I became unexpectedly ill. But mother knew what was wrong with me. I felt faint and dizzy and was always vomiting. She just said gently, "inshallah, it is good". Saeid rushed me off to hospital. I lay on the bed and looked up at Saeid, who was full of concern. The doctor told Saeid to wait outside until he was called. I was overcome with a strange weakness and was struggling to keep my eyes open. The doctor then asked if I could answer some questions to which I nodded. After he had asked his questions and examined me, he called Saeid back in.

He said, "don't worry. It's nothing dreadful. It's just that you will become a father soon. Your wife had low blood pressure because of the vomiting. Now take this prescription to the pharmacy and return. Then Saeid's concern turned into a broad smile. He came to me and congratulated me.

" You will become a mother soon," he said joyfully. And off he went to get the medicine for me.

My eyes were warm and my mind empty of any ideas. Later, I felt the prick of a needle injecting the serum. Saeid was back and he told me to sleep, and he would return when the effects of the serum had worn off. I don't know how many hours I slept for, but eventually I was able to leave the hospital and go home with Saeid's help, after thanking the doctor and nurse.

Summer died in the wrath of autumn wind. All the leaves from the trees were on the ground. The brittle sound under our shoes was like bones breaking, a damaging of destiny. Saeid now understood why his mother hadn't been worried about me; she knew it meant she was going to be a grandmother; she had experience and had recognized the signs.

"Shall we get the pastries to celebrate. Will you agree to present the pastries and make the announcement about our news to mother and father?"

I approved by nodding my head. I was confused and only heard the half of what Saeid was saying. It was a big load on my shoulders and smiles and tears mixed together for me at that moment. Could I cope with this great responsibility of becoming a parent? In that moment, I had a picture of my own mother in my head, as she wiped away the tears with the corner of her scarf, instead of smiling. Saeid broke into my thoughts with his excited call for me to come and see. I hadn't noticed but we had now arrived at the confectionary shop.

"Which ones should we buy?"

We purchased the pastries and went home., When Saeid's mother heard the news, she was so thrilled – it was like her lips had become full of pink flowers. She hugged and kissed me. By now it was lunch time. After changing my clothes, I hurried to the kitchen to cook the meal.

But Mother said kindly, "I will cook. You are tired today; you should rest."

I was a bit worried and asked her, "are you concerned about me, or your grandchild?"

She said both, for me and for her grandchild.

I hugged her and said I wasn't sure what my mother would have done now.

She hugged me back and said soothingly, "now you are with me. Don't you believe me I will look after you like my own daughter?"

I wiped away my tears which had mixed with my eye make-up in a very unattractive way and said, "I'm sorry, it's just that this news today has made me think about my mother, and all the many wishes she had for me. She won't ever know how it all turned out".

She replied, "there are many different paths in life, who knows where they will lead? One day your mother might get to see her grandchild."

I let out a loud sigh and said, "I hope so".

When Saeid came, I changed the subject so I wouldn't make him even more tired. I put the cookies on a dish and went with Saeid to father, who had just come home. He was very happy to hear the news and a look of great joy spread across his face.

From that day, I became the dear one. Lina came to visit me two or three times a week. She cooked for me the food I craved to eat during my pregnancy. And mother's kindness to me was unlimited. She didn't let me do anything.

***

It was early in July. There was a lot of warmth in the sun and the weather was hot and harsh.

By now I had grown to be quite huge, waiting for the child who had grown inside me to be born. My time had drawn near; everyone was waiting. Right at the end of that month, the waiting came to an end. My baby was born after what was for me, a painful birth. He was a chubby baby boy with black eyes like Saeid's and a round plump face like mine. The happiness of Saeid and his family was another blessing. We named him Vahid. A naming ceremony was held for my dear boy. I had high hopes for his future. I promised myself to be a good mother, stay with him and defend him.

Chapter 7

My child isolated me from my previous world. Everything from my past was wiped from my mind, except my mother. I thought of her smiles, and all that she did for me that had eventually led me to freedom, and to my new life with Saeid.

The economic problems in our simple household remained unsolved. We had all come to accept it and were no longer looking for solutions. The loneliness that came from the exile from our own land was the overriding factor in our lives, and the unsatisfactory nature of Saeid's and his father's jobs made life more difficult. Every day Saeid did a job that did not suit him, was contrary to his nature and to his education. I had previously been used to a harsh life and was somewhat more content with our small income and had no complaints. But I still continued to look for a better job for Saeid to improve our situation. The more I searched, the less I found.

***

Seven years later, and it was close to sunset, mother had cleaned the house and washed the walls to make the hot July weather feel more tolerable. I made tea and waited for my husband, while Vahid talked to me and amused me.

He said, "mother, do I go to school this year?"

I patted him gently on the head as I sat in front of him, looked into his black and bold eyes and said surely, "of course, you're seven now, you're old enough to start school".

I had concerns for my child. Would he become successful? Could he take his rightful place in society? Was that an unattainable goal? In other skies, how much further might he be able to fly? Where could we go to make that goal a possibility?

The ring of the doorbell distracted my thoughts. Vahid ran to welcome his father. But returned and said, Kaka Samei has come, mother. I said to myself 'now, alone'? I went to see what was going on. I saw Samei talking to mother. Mother was pale and worried. She hadn't yet seen me and was saying slowly, "Roya? How will we be able to tell her?". I begged her to tell me what had happened? But nobody knew what to say. Nobody said anything - Samei and mother were crying. I was going crazy with worry.

I shouted, "what happened? Someone talk. Tell me now."

Mother tried to cover up her sadness. She took Vahid and went into the other room.

I went to Samei and said, "please, for god's sake, tell me what happened? I'm concerned".

Samei said, "don't worry".

I interrupted, begging him to give me the details.

After a short pause he said, "Saeid is at the hospital".

On hearing these words, my world turned around in my head and I went blank. When I opened my eyes again, it was like I could feel the pain of the serum needle against my arm. I remembered what Samei had just said and was overwhelmed with anxiety for my beloved Saeid. I pulled myself together and rushed out of the room in a passion.

Lina ran to me and said, "why are you rushing around like this? You'll do yourself some harm. Think of your child. You should be resting."

***

At the hospital I couldn't take it all in. I opened the door of the room to look for my missed one. Lina was talking with the nurse. I could see her lips moving but could hear nothing.

The nurse stood firmly in front of me barring the way, looked me straight in the eye, and said, "your husband is not here. He is undergoing surgery on the fifth floor".

I broke down and cried inconsolably. Lina came close, seeing me in need of a shoulder to continue crying on. She hugged me and I emptied myself of tears on her shoulder.

I passed along endless hospital corridors until finally, at one end, I saw Saeid's father looking very anxious.

He said, with a worried voice, "he has been in surgery now for four hours and nothing is known. I couldn't answer but went to Samei who was sitting on a bench.

I said, "hello Samei," and he looked up at me, his tired face telling me that he had had no sleep last night.

He asked me if I was feeling better now, but I was still confused and asked him angrily, "how did this happened?"

He said, "this isn't the right time. I will tell you later".

I said angrily, "I should know now," and he saw then that I wasn't going to take no for an answer and agreed to tell me it all.

Lina and I sat and listened carefully.

He said, "yesterday we didn't have a good start., In the morning, Master Ali, our rude supervisor was in a bad mood and humiliated us in front of the others. The Afghan workers, as always, were working under worse conditions than the others. He called us all 'damn Afghans'. Me and Saeid didn't confront him then but waited until our work was finished. We had already changed our clothes when Master Ali told Saeid one of the scaffold poles on the third floor weren't right and that he should go and fix it. Saeid told him it was too dark, and that he would fix it the next morning. Master Ali said, 'do what I said, you fucking Afghan!' Saeid was red with anger and was ready to fight, But I said 'no, you'll lose your job',He saw the logic in that and accepted it, so off he went. He took his toolsand went back up there in the dark. But soon after that I heard a crash andI saw him lying there on the ground, all covered in blood. His foot had slipped on the bars, and he had fallen. There were no tears for Saeid's sacrifice."

I said, interrupting him, "he never got used to this job; he hated it but never complained. He did it because of us, because we needed the money to live."

We continued talking and cried dead rivers of tears. Everyone was tired and sad as we sat there waiting. Suddenly, looking around I realised that mother wasn't here. I asked Lina where she was, and she told me that she had stayed home to look after the children. Vahid! How would I ever find the words to explain this to him? I asked for God's guidance on what I should do?

Father said to Lina, "daughter go to the house. Your girl is small; she needs milk. Care for Vahid and your daughter and let mother come here. She needs to be here for her son."

Lina said goodbye and went home while we continued to wait for the surgery door to open. Waiting was harder than drinking venom. The second hand of the white clock on the wall seemed to be hardly moving. Why was time passing so slowly? When was this ever going to end? What to do with my tired body while I waited to find out the fate of my beloved? This waiting was killing me. Father's insistence on eating breakfast made me crazy. He kept giving me food and trying to get me to eat it, due to modesty, I made no objection to his efforts. But then the door opened and I was free of father's importunities as, along with everyone else, I ran towards the doctor as he came out of the surgery.

Samei and I said together, "hello doctor. How is our patient"?

He said politely, "we've done all we can, the rest is in God's hands now. There is some serious damage done to the skull. I am hoping he will wake up soon."

I asked, "can I see him?"

He said, "yes, when he has been moved to the ward. But now you must go home and rest, and return again at visiting hour."

Mother who had returned in the last few minutes said, "I'm not tired. I will wait here and go with him to the ward. You go home and get some rest."

We tried to forget about the tired and injured body of Saeid for a while, and returned home feeling desperate.

Vahid opened the door for us and asked immediately, "where is father Saeid?"

I hugged him and told him that he was a little ill at the moment, so he would be staying at the hospital for a few days more.

Father asked him for a hug and said, "let's go and eat while we wait for visiting time".

His manly pride wouldn't allow him to show the emotion he was feeling, but I saw how he cried when the others weren't around.

Lina and Samei took their daughter and said goodbye and went home. I was left with this enormous hole inside of me that was filled with sadness. I went up the stairs slowly; everywhere I could smell the scent of my beloved Saeid, the smell of love. He was in a battle for survival and the conditions were unfavourable for him. I took his picture from the wall, kissed it and pressed it against my heart. I threw my body down on the bed covered with the red flowered rug. The picture in its frame became wet in the rain of my tears. But then I heard Vahid coming, and I quickly wiped my tears away.

"Mother, mother, look what grandfather has bought for me?"

I kissed him and said, "did you remember to thank your dear grandfather?"

Father became aware of the picture frame in my hand. He took it slowly from me and put it back on the wall without looking.

Then he whispered in my ear, "be careful. The child doesn't understand your sadness. In Saeid's absence you have a double duty. Be strong my dear bride, you have seen worse days."

I nodded to let father know I had understood his words and tried to pull myself together. I asked him what he would like for lunch?

A bitter smile appeared on his face as he told me to cook whatever Vahid wanted today. Then he rolled up his sleeves and went to perform his ablutions.

Vahid sat in front of the TV with father beside him. I asked what he would like me to do for lunch? He said he would like some pasta, and I left him to watch his cartoon, while I went to prepare the meal.

***

His cold hands seemed to suck all the warmth from my own hands. There were still signs of blood on his face.

I bent my head slowly towards his ear and said, "dear Saeid, dear Saeid". But there was not even the smallest of a sign of his waking up. It was like he was in a deep, deep sleep. The tears coursing down my cheeks dropped onto him, but still he did not move.

"Saeid, please wake up and let me see your eyes once more. What answer can I give to our son? Don't leave me alone. You promised to be with me forever. Please wake up for God's sake."

The nurse complained that I was making too much noise.

"Dear lady, he can hear nothing. Please leave now or go to visit the next person."

I kissed the cold hand of Saeid and left the room. My world was on that bed.

I passed by everyone carelessly. I saw nobody. My legs seemed to be dragging me along without me willing them to. I suddenly realised I had made my way to Saeid's place of work. I looked at myself and realized that my clothes were trailing in the dust and had got quite dirty. I raised my veil out of the dirt and tidied myself up as best I could.

I approached one of the workers there and asked him in his language, "Who do you work for? Who is your supervisor?"

He called loudly, "master... master, they want you".

A dirty-looking man came close and said, "I am Master Ali. What do you want, sister?"

I said, "I am Saeid's wife, your worker who was injured last week as a result of your actions".

He replied very rudely, "so what?"

I said, "you know he has not yet regained consciousness?"

He said, "I heard something about that".

I hid my tears and said, "if my son has no father, if Saeid doesn't regain consciousness, what will you do, then?"

He sneered, "what is that to us? He isn't one of us?"

I said, "if you hadn't made him angry with the way you humiliated him, and hadn't sent him up there in the dark, then this wouldn't have happened".

He smiled and said, "don't be sad now. If your husband dies, I'd be a good father for your son".

I was very angry. I didn't know what this idiot thought he was. I raised my hand and slapped him hard. He then retaliated, kicking me and telling me to go away, or he would call the police to come and take me away.

I fell to the ground, weak and with my clothes getting even more dirty. Full of tears I wanted to shout and rage at him.

All their blood gathered in the faces of the Afghan workers as they raged within themselves, but fear of losing their jobs made them hold their peace. They came close and raised me up and guided me back outside of the half constructed building. One of them got me a taxi, like a kind brother, and told the driver where to take me.

He said, "go sister, don't talk with this godless person. Pray for Saeid's health. Inshallah, he wakes up soon and returns to you and your son".

I said, "thank you brother, but go back quickly or you will lose your job".

The taxi moved off, leaving behind the people who seemed to be laughing at me like I was some sort of street clown. I said to myself, 'God, where are these people and where am I? What a question. I couldn't think about it. I felt like I was homeless, always having to move on, no real place to stay. I shouted out that the dream was over, the good days all gone. The sound of driver telling me we had arrived pulled me from this sadness.

I thanked him and walked towards the house. In the walls of that old alley, I could see reflected memories of Saeid. My tired steps took me to the wooden door. I knocked and Vahid opened the door. He said 'hello' and hugged me.

"Where were you mother?"

Mother came close and asked me, "where were you, daughter? We were very afraid and thought of a thousand things that might have happened".

"Don't be worried about me. What could happen to me?"

"Please stop for god's sake; if you became ill, what about this child?"

"Ok, OK, but what news is there from the hospital?"

"Nothing since you left. We visited Saeid one by one and talked to the doctor."

" And what did the doctor say?"

"He just repeated what he said earlier."

I took off my dirty veil, and went and changed my robe. While I was washing I said, "but I know Saeid will wake up. He would never leave me alone".

I splashed the cold water over my face and head, then took off my socks and washed my feet at the fountain. The tiredness seemed to slowly dissolve into the water. When I felt more relaxed, I went to Vahid, who was gently leaning against the wall, watching me. I picked him up, giving him a hug and then carried him into the living room where Father was drinking tea. I said 'hello' and put Vahid back down on the ground. As usual, Mother's samovar was full, its contents already boiling. I went over, lowered the flame and made two cups of green tea for mother and me, and then joined them.

Father said, "where did you go when you left the hospital dear girl?"

I didn't want to bother him by telling him about what had happened with Master Ali and just said, "I went for a walk; I needed to be alone".

Mother then said, "can you come to the market with me in the morning?"

"Yes, we can go in the morning. After visiting Saeid we will go together."

I then asked father if he had investigated what the registration conditions were for Vahid to go to school?

"Yes, I went to the local school, and they wrote down the required documents for me," he told me.

"So what documents do we need?"

Father got up and took a piece of paper from the pocket of his old coat that was hanging on a nail in the wall and gave it to me. It said it required a letter from Chahar Chesmeh along with one hundred and fifty in toman money, and other documents for registration. I looked at the paper and asked him where Chahar Cheshmeh was.

"It is a place outside the city. It is very busy. One citizen said there is a long queue and you need to go at night to secure your place in it."

"And nothing can be done about it so I shall have to go one day and get this letter. Vahid should be included in school this year, and we will have to save the money, anyway."

Mother said, "God is mighty, have patience".

Our life is full of patience, otherwise we are nothing.

Vahid had fallen asleep on my feet. My legs were burning. I gently released my foot from under him and massaged it to bring it back to life. I rubbed my leg as I talked to father, and asked him if it wasn't too difficult, if we could determine a day for him to go to Chahar Cheshmeh to get that letter.

"Of course my girl, I will think about it."

Mother told me that if I was afraid of being alone in the night, I could sleep here, but I told them I wasn't afraid.

I hugged Vahid, said 'goodnight' and went to our room.

I put Vahid in his bed. I saw there was a lot of dust in the house, like nobody had been living there in a while. After Saeid's accident, I had had no motivation for housework. I ignored it and went to bed. Vahid was soon asleep, his black eyes closed under the veil of his dark lashes, and his lips rosy pink under the red light of the lamp.

I was uncertain about the future of my child. If Saeid left me alone, then what would happen? No … no, thinking about it was just too dreadful. I would be right back in my fatherless days, a girl without any support. I didn't want that destiny for Vahid. I promised myself that night that I would fight to the death to prevent that happening, fight for Vahid's comfort and forget about my own wants and desires. Eventually my eyes became heavy and I slept dreaming of my innocent son's face.

***

The warm weather was difficult. I could feel drops of sweat running down my back. The pungent smell of sweat offended my nose. I wished it wasn't from me. I cared less about myself in those days. I looked out of the window on the bus and saw the signs.

Mother said, "dear Roya, we've arrived. We need to get off the bus here".

We got off and I entered the jewellery shop with mother.

Mother put all her jewels on the table and said, "please weigh these; I want to sell them".

I whispered to her, "wait a little longer. God is mighty, He might yet provide the money".

She shook her head and said "don't you see? They said if we don't pay the hospital bill in the morning, no matter how ill Saeid is, they will evict him from the hospital".

I remembered, then, the doctor saying if you don't have money, why bother? Saeid is brain dead and will never wake up. Be satisfied and donate his organs, so others may survive from certain death.

Then Saeid's mother had said, "we will pay the hospital. My son is alive, I am not happy to donate his organs".

We had hurried home and got the jewellery and come straight here to raise the money. The man put a wad of money down on the table and from it mother took some and handed it to me.

She said, "take this one hundred and fifty thousand tomans, Roya, for Vahid's school."

I said desperately, "I am not satisfied….". Then I stopped what I was going to say and instead said, "mother… if this was passed down to me, I would have no use for gold and jewellery if I don't have Saeid. This is meant to be for use in hard times and what day could possibly be harder than today?"

We went directly from the jewellery store to the hospital to pay the bill, then went to see Saeid in his room. His weak body was on the bed and there were many systems attached to him.

I went forward slowly and said, "hello, dear Saeid, I know you can hear my voice. We are all good. Vahid wanted to come but children aren't allowed here".

Then I bent closer and kissed his face, which was not looking so bruised and bloody now. But like all the other days there was no reaction. He was like a dead man. I wondered to myself how long we could go on visiting him like this. The Nurse interrupted, "you are his wife?"

"Yes," and I pointed to mother and said, "and she is his mother".

She gave me a dish that contained a white talcum-powder like substance and said, "you need to rub this powder on the sides and back of the patient. He has been laying on this bed for a long time and he has developed bed-sores where the bed has been chaffing his skin."

With mother's help, I turned Saeid on his side, and after removing the sheet that was covering him, I saw that in several places his skin was red and blistered which looked very painful. No-one could tolerate those conditions. We cried as we applied the powder to the sores and then turned him over so that he was laying on his other side.

Mother looked at me and said, "how is this going to end, Roya?"

"I don't know. I only know that if he stays in this bed any longer, he won't have any healthy skin left on his body. You stay with him for now and I'll go and talk with his doctor".

I knocked on the door of the doctor's office and when he called, I entered.

"Hello, doctor."

"Hello lady, what can I do for you?"

I sat on the warm black couch there and then asked, "Doctor, when will Saeid's condition change?"

"Whenever you want."

"What does that mean?"

"Let's speak candidly; it is your right to know his condition. As I told you before, Saeid is brain dead. The neurons inside his brain are not functioning – they are dead, and he has no response. He can't breathe unaided. His condition is irreversible, He will not get better. It is not a kindness to keep him like this. You should accept the reality. Allow us to switch off the life support machinery. By donating his organs, the heart you loved will live on in another body."

The lips of the doctor still moved, but I heard nothing. Everything started to go black. The room and everything in it were revolving. It was like riding on a merry go round on a dark night. I felt weak and powerless as I began to slip away. I couldn't understand my condition.

"Lady … lady … are you alright?"

That was the sound of the nurse in my head. Mother was handing me a glass of sweet water but I hardly noticed. Slowly I opened my eyes and moved the glass away from my face and said "I am OK … OK".

Mother said, "what did the doctor say to you that made you so bad?" How could I answer that look? I had to be silent, and said nothing.

Mother took hold of me under my arm and slowly helped me towards the hospital's garden. A cold breeze touched my face and my eyes opened wide.

She sat me down on a bench there and said, "I'm going to buy some fruit juice. Your blood pressure has certainly dropped".

I followed her tired steps with my eyes. This will be devastating for her. I remembered years ago when my mother and I had hankered after the sort of relaxed life that our neighbours enjoyed. Now that happy Faezeh was replaced with this sad mother and her lips no longer smiled so easily. What had she done to deserve this pain? There were many Faezehs, walking down life's alleys of pain. I thought to myself, 'how can I tell this news to the others?' I couldn't do it. I got up and slowly walked to the phone kiosk and dialled a number.

"This is Doctor Moeini. How can I help you."

"Hello doctor, I am the wife of Saeid, the patient in room 112.

"Ok, speak please."

"I wanted to ask you if you could inform Saeid's father and mother of this bad news, like you told me."

"Ok. I will inform them tomorrow. You will think about the donation?"

"I said before, I won't allow you to cut my husband's body up."

"I understand. I had a duty to suggest it to you, though."

"Goodbye doctor."

I hung up the phone. Mother was by the bench looking for me. I went towards her.

"Where were you, Roya?"

I answered her kind voice with a smile and said, "I went to drink some water".

She gave me the juice she had bought and said, "drink, It will make you feel better".

***

The golden light of the sun was under my eyelids. I slowly opened my eyes. I wished that I didn't have to see a morning without Saeid. The light reflected on the white face of Vahid. I pulled my tired body out from under the covers and got up carefully so as not to disturb my son.

I went over to the window and adjusted the curtain to prevent the sunlight from shining on Vahid's face. I looked at the geranium beside the window; it was dried up and looked half-dead. But when the flower of my life laid prisoned in the tubes and wires at the hospital, the geranium on the window was forgotten.

I took a watering pot and watered the poor dried-up flower in memory of Saeid. The mirror on the wall reflected the great sadness on my face. The signs of youth were still obvious under the dark veil of pain. In this year I became twenty seven. I asked myself, 'is it my destiny to suffer such pain? The voice of the doctor echoed in my ears - 'you should accept the reality'. Saeid is not alive; it is just these devices that give him breath. Could I really become a widow at this young age? I said to myself, you fought hard to change your destiny, but the legacy of your mother was an eternal bond with sadness.

I splashed water on my face, and the coolness of it added to my tears, so that I became calm again. That day I was supposed to go to Chahar Cheshmeh to get the letter for Vahid's school. I put on my clothes and joined Saeid's father and mother for breakfast.

"Hello, good morning."

Father said, "hello my girl, come eat breakfast and then we will go".

Mother said, "shall we get a taxi?"

Father said, "no woman, I have borrowed a motorcycle from my friend. In these conditions, spending one less thousand toman is essential".

I said, "that's a good idea".

Mother took a sip of her tea and said, "I told Lina she should go to the hospital today to ask about her brother. I will stay home and take care of the children".

I put cheese and vegetable on my bread and said, "thank you mother; what should I do without you?"

Mother said, "you would still have God and he is much more powerful".

Father smiled and said, "stop the compliments. Roya, my girl, eat your breakfast soon or you will be late".

After breakfast, father and I sat together on the old motorcycle that father had borrowed, although he suffered dreadfully from the shame he felt for having to do so. He set off slowly.

I said that if he carried on driving that slowly we wouldn't even get there by nightfall.

He replied that he had to be careful, as the motorcycle was on loan, and also that we should pray that we wouldn't be stopped for his license to be checked or because we weren't wearing crash helmets. God would help us, he added.

Near noon we had reached Chahar Cheshmeh. It was a suburb of Mashhad. There was a long queue and there were many poor people sitting on the ground in the hot sun.

A woman wearing a flowery scarf and a dusty veil said, "I am the last one. You should stand behind me"

I nodded my head in agreement and asked her if she, too, had come for the school letter?

She said, "Yes. I have three children at school. This year, to raise the money we needed, we sold our carpet. My husband is a simple worker, and barely earns enough money to pay for our food and other necessities."

I said, "don't be sad, mother. It is a curse on all Afghans".

Meanwhile a sound came from the front of the queue. I asked the man in charge what had happened.

"A woman who has been waiting here since morning prayer has fainted from thirst and hunger. This happens at least two or three times every day."

I turned to father and said, "we are going to be waiting for a long time here. It's better you go home now, and come back for me at sunset".

He said, "I can't leave you alone in this desert".

I pointed to the long line of people waiting and said, "I am not alone, there is a huge crowd here."

With a little more persuading, I finally convinced him that he should leave. After he left, it was just me waiting. I got tired of standing and sat on an old carton beside the other woman. Time passed slowly. She told me her whole life story. I had no answers I could give to her and only nodded my head here and there in confirmation. There was chaos welling up inside me. I thought to myself 'this woman's husband is alive in this city and yet she still has all these problems. How on earth am I going to manage life without Saeid?' The sun was at its zenith and radiated vertically down on us all. I was hungry and thirsty.

I looked at the woman and said, "mother please keep my place so I can go and get something to eat." I didn't wait for an answer and started to move, but she took my hand and said she wouldn't allow it. She had some bread, fat yoghurt and vegetables. She insisted we could share the food. Her generous behavior made me feel ashamed.

I said I couldn't accept, but she smiled and said, "think of me like I am your mother; when I say sit, just say yes. Don't you know they sell the food here at an extortionate price because they know we have no choice. They take advantage of our situation."

She took my hand, and I sat down there on the earth next to her. As she said, I felt safe, like a daughter with her mother. She opened her small food pack which was an old scarf decorated with yellow flowers. A bowl of fat yoghurt, fresh vegetable and bread, a flask of tea and two glasses. All from her woven pack.

It was close to 2 o'clock, I was waiting eagerly. There were only two people in front of me, and then it would be my turn.

The woman looked at me and said, "finally it is my turn".

She moved forward and got ready to hand her documents through the glass partition between her and the agents inside the building.

But then the agent said, "the time is over, we have finished for the day. Go and come back again tomorrow".

The woman begged them to process her papers before they closed, but the agent insisted that work was over for the day and repeated that she would have to come back tomorrow. The woman became pale. It was the worst news in her life.

"Brother," she said, "my way is long, I paid a lot of money for the taxi and bus to get here today. God won't like it if I return empty handed."

But the man had a tough character, and didn't care about her cries.

I took her shoulder and said, "it's OK. Let's go ", but she insisted, and didn't move her hand away from the glass.

I said to the agent, "we will return tomorrow but this woman has a problem. Do her papers, for God's sake. Without paying any attention to me, he closed the window on the woman's fingers. She cried out in pain. With the help of others, we managed to release the woman's hand from the glass shutter. Her fingers were bruised, and she had tears in her eyes. I treated her hand with some cream I had in my bag and bandaged it with a towel. I then took her by the shoulders and sat her by a corner of the building.

I joined the rest of the people who had been left in the queue and we all moved to the entrance to the building to object about what the agents had done.

I turned to the agent and said, "what you have just done is illegal. You shouldn't hurt people".

The agent sneered and aid, "I was waiting for you to come and teach me the law". And to the crowd he said, "it is what it is. If you don't like it return to your own damn country".

I shook my head slowly with sorrow and returned to where I had left the woman. But she was gone. She had gone to fight new problems.

After an hour of waiting, father came for me. On the way home I told him the story of what had happened. He said that some people had no sense of humanity. There was no need for me to return in the morning. He insisted he would go by himself.

"I know how to behave towards them," he finished.

I thought of that woman continuously. Would her children get to study this year? Would she conquer or lose? And a thousand other questions were going through my head. It was like my own miseries were lost in the sad story of that woman.

***

It was completely dark when we reached home. When I saw the real face of father under the light of the lamp in the backyard, I knew he had his concerns about Saeid. I thought that Dr Moeini had probably talked to him, too. I didn't care and went directly to my room. Vahid was asleep. I bent down slowly and kissed his beautiful face. I washed my dirty and dusty clothes and joined the others in the living room. I saw Nafise, Lina's daughter, crawling in front of the door, so I knew Lina was still there. Lina and Samei stood up in respect, and I welcomed them with kindness. I went to see mother in the kitchen; everything was arranged, the food was already in the oven, and the salad was ready inside the fridge. But there was no sign of mother. For a moment I was afraid, and rushed back to Lina to askwhere mother was.

She paused for a second and then said, "at the hospital".

"Well… she stayed with Saeid?"

"No … I don't know. Ask father."

Father was alone with God in the backyard. I went to him there and saw himpraying.

"God what should I do? My son in the hospital is dying, and my wife is in pain and suffering, Show me the way."

My tears flowed down my face, and I returned without bothering him. I told Lina that I knew everything, and she didn't need to hide it, that the doctor had talked to me yesterday. Lina had been restraining herself until now, hiding her tears from me. She told me then that when mother had heard it, she couldn't stand it and had had a seizure and was now in the hospital as well.

I said, "I should go to her. Dear Samei, can you take me?"

"It is nighttime now, there is no visiting until tomorrow."

"But I should go, I can't wait until morning."

"OK. Go and get ready."

***

At the hospital entrance, I implored the guard for hours to let us inside. Eventually, I was allowed in and went to mother's room. She had many devices attached to her.

I called to her quietly. "mother… dear mother".

She turned her face towards me, and I could see her eyes were tired. She looked very sad.

I went closer and said, "hello", and she asked me if I had got Vahid's school letter.?

"No… my turn wasn't reached before they closed for the day. Father goes in the morning. Don't be worried."

"I don't want Saeid to be worried about the future of his son. You heard the news? They want me to send my son to be sacrificed, to give every part of his body to someone else, but I won't allow it; my son is alive and breathing."

"Mother, think about your own health. I swear to God, Saeid would not be happy to see you in this condition."

But then the nurse came in and interrupted us, screaming "who let you in? Don't you know the rules?"

"Miss, there's no need to humiliate me. I am just leaving."

I kissed mother's face and returned home with Samei. My little child was still free from all concerns and slept peacefully. But I couldn't sleep. My mind was full of Saeid, the sadness fell over my head. From the moment the doctor had told me about Saeid, he had been my only thought. At night, I waited patiently in the darkness for morning to come. During the day I was preparing Vahid for the day he would become a fatherless child.

***

Father was a realistic and kind man. One day after mother had recovered, he took us to visit the heart patients who were in the hospital. Our pain was enormous, but the pain of those waiting for death increased the tone of pain in our souls. There was one girl there, who had taken off her purple scarf so that her head was uncovered exposing her silky brown hair, and her beautiful eyes shining through the dark shadows. Her tiny frail-looking hand was on her mother, and she was talking to her sweetly. This attracted my attention to her, and after asking for her permission, I sat down beside her bed.

"Hello, we came to visit the patients."

"Welcome."

"I am Roya."

"My name is Arezoo."

"Wow, what a beautiful name. How old are you, Arezoo."

"Seventeen."

"Unless I am mistaken, you are from Afghanistan?"

"Yes, from Ghandhar province; we came here for treatment."

I turned to look at her mother and saw how sad she looked. I asked how long Arezoo had been waiting for an organ donation?

"One and a half years," her mother replied.

"I don't think it will be her turn soon. We've done everything we can, but nothing has done any good. She gets worse every day. I don't know what to do."

"God is bigger than our imagination. Have hope. Maybe she will be more fortunate than you think."

"I don't have any doubts in God, I am just so tired."

I didn't allow her to talk any more about sadness. I just kissed her face and said goodbye.

I could see that mother was still reluctant to make the decision to switch off Saeid's life support system.

I said, "you see that girl? She is Arezoo from Ghandhar. According to the law here it is not possible to donate to Afghans".

These words shook her to the core. She looked at her husband and said with tears in her eyes, "I will sign the consent form and donate Saeid's heart to Arezoo".

Father said, "if the doctor and hospital allow it."

After visiting the heart patients, we saw the doctor. Mother said we would sign the consent form if her son's organs could be given to foreign patients and his heart could be given to Arezoo.

The doctor smiled and said, "I am happy with your decision - it is the right thing to do. We want to save lives and I'm sorry that it has worked out like this for you".

The consent form was signed, and it was agreed that the machinery would be switched off the next day. I wanted some time with my husband and asked the doctor if I could spend that last night with Saeid. He forwarded my request to the nurse. Mother and father left the room, and I was left with Saeid's half-dead body. I was fearful and alone. I searched my beloved's face for any sign of his innocent smile, but he kept sleeping. The curved lines on the device showing that he was still alive, although his heart no longer beat for me.

The environment of the hospital … me and Saeid alone in his room as I whispered words of love … so similar, yet so different to those early days. He was like a saving angel for me; he came to rescue me from death and freed me from the desperation of my former life. He released me from the soulless world I lived in and showed me the way of love in life. Now this bird of fortune had left me in silence, to travel diverging paths to different destinies. He was going to leave me behind with this overwhelming sadness. My heart wrenched, as I took his cold hand to say goodbye.

***

Dear Saeid, now you have chosen your destination, and I am all alone, what should I do? When I used to say I am alone, you would answer, 'don't say that. I am with you, have no sadness'. Remember? But now there is nothing but sadness going through my head, what can I do? I am left with this innocent child. How can I be both father and mother to him? It is too big of a responsibility for me; the weight on my back is too heavy. All of this talk, but his only answer was silence.

It was morning, but the fog hid the sun. I kissed the Quran, closed it and put it on the bedside table near Saeid's head. The backyard was suddenly lonely for me. I splashed my face with water and looked in the mirror. A Roya full of sadness looked back at me. I went back in and slept beside his bed with no regard for my own comfort and watched him. Eventually the clock on the wall showed that it was 8 am and the door opened and Vahid came in.

"Hello mother."

"Hello son? Where did you come from?"

"Everyone came and I was with them."

He went to Saeid's bed and said, "hello dad, are you all right?"

My son had come to see his dad for the last time. I was choked by the sadness in the room and the cry in my throat. I forced myself not to cry for my son's sake.

I went to Vahid, sat and took his hands and said, "dear son you should say goodbye to your father today".

"Where is he going?"

"To God?"

"Do you mean now I will have no father like Hasan, the son of our neighbour?"

I couldn't stand it and the tears coursed down my face as I said, "you have me and I will be both a father and mother to you, so don't be sad".

He said, crying, "but I want dad".

I said, "but we have to say goodbye to him. Do it now because the others are waiting."

He kissed Saeid with his tiny lips and said, "father, please don't go. Stay if you can. I will miss you."

I took him by the shoulder and directed him towards the door. All the members of the family were waiting behind the door to say goodbye, one by one. After greeting them, I left them with Saeid and removed Vahid from the room. I sat on a bench beside a big pine tree and watched Vahid playing in the yard. The playground in the backyard made him forget about his loss temporarily. He was just a child at play without a care in the world. It took me back to my childhood. I was reminded of my father's mourning ceremony. I didn't know then that it would be the beginning of all my miseries. I hid my tears and asked myself what Vahid's destiny would be. Why did he also have to become fatherless? Was this some sort of test of destiny for me?

Lina's voice distracted me from my lonely thoughts.

"Roya, Roya, come. Saeid is being transferred to the operating theatre."

I took Vahid's hand and hurried back to Saeid's room. All the members of our family were there in one corner, sad and crying. Saeid's bed was being taken by two nurses towards the operating theatre. Vahid was handed to his aunt, and I hurried after Saeid.

"Wait a little, I want to say goodbye once more. Goodbye Saeid, I'll see you in heaven. I promise to protect our son as you would wish."

Saeid was wheeled away along the hospital corridor, as my happiness was taken away with him. I sat on the ground and wept. A hand touched my shoulder.

" God give you patience."

I turned my head towards the sound. It was Arezoo's mother - Arezoo, the girl from Ghandhar. Her eyes were sad like mine. I hadn't slept all night and was too exhausted to get up, but she helped me sit down. When I was a little more relaxed, I asked her what she was doing there?

She said, "the surgery for Arezoo and your husband are at the same time. It was like a miracle. When I heard what you had done, I knew there are still good people in this world. You only need to open your eyes."

I said, "I give Saeid's heart to you. He had a kind heart. Surely it will work well for your girl."

She wanted to kiss my hand, but I wouldn't let her.

***

The surgery was successful; the life taken from Saeid was gifted to Arezoo. After thirty-six hours we took Saeid's body and buried it with respect.

The third, seventh and fortieth mourning days were held. I was sunk inside myself with grief - the sadness of being a widow with a fatherless child. I went with the others to pray, according to tradition, my lips forgot how to smile, and my eyes would never forget the tears. My life was suspended, and my son was the only entity of my world.

***

Maybe my will to write ended then, too. Now who would I write for? Who would teach me and encourage me like a wise master? Yes, by burying Saeid, I forgot about writing. I didn't want to write about how to raise my son in poverty and as an exile in a foreign land.

Goodbye.

Chapter 8

Under the light of the study lamp, I cried silently. Roya's memoirs were left unfinished, and I wanted to know the rest of her sad story. Reading it had reminded me of my own childhood. The neighbour on the other side of the fig river had been a beautiful girl and they had said she was lost. They mourned and treated her as if she was a dead girl. By coincidence her name was Roya. I had a feeling about the relationship between this Roya and that young dead girl. The name of their father and brothers was the same. Also, the style of life. It all made me curious to explore more. I rested my chin on my hands as I sat there and continued to think. The sound of Farhad's voice distracted me, and I turned in my chair to look at him.

Yawning, he said in his broken English, "Homa, don't you want to sleep, it is past 3 am".

Then I realised how long I had spent reading Roya's memories. I said I would come, but first I should take a bath.

While I was taking my bath and brushing my teeth, I thought about the connection between the two Royas, but came to no conclusion and wondered why a mother would consider her girl as dead? Was it possible that this was the same girl? I must have asked myself this a thousand times, but still could not come up with an answer. I couldn't think straight because of my extreme tiredness; my brain wouldn't work. I went to bed and slept beside Farhad dreaming of the Seven Kingdoms. I closed my eyes; sleep stopped any chance of thinking.

I woke up to the sound of the alarm clock. But my eyes were full of the tiredness from last night. They didn't want to open. I wanted to shut the sound out by thrusting the clock under my pillow, but Farhad knew my habit and had placed the clock on the other side of the room to prevent me from doing it. So, I had to get up out of bed to turn it off. By then I was fully awake and had lost the urge to sleep. Farhad had made breakfast. From his shaved face, I could tell that he had already had a bath.

"Hello, Mr Early Riser."

"Hello, Lady Sleepyhead. Get over here - breakfast is ready."

I washed my hands and face and joined Farhad at the table. He placed my breakfast down and asked me what I planned to do that day.

I thought of Roya and without thinking about how strange it would sound I said, "is it possible to have a daughter who is alive even though you say she is dead?"

"Since when do you answer a question with another question?"

"You answer first …"

"Where and in which culture?"

"Isn't it obvious - Afghanistan of course."

"It happens a lot in Afghanistan. Sometimes when a girl is lost, they think she is dead. And sometimes if she runs away from home, they say she is dead because of fears for their reputation. Why do you ask?"

Keeping secrets was one of the principles of my job. I jumped up in a hurry and said I should go, I was late.

I got dressed and as I left the house I said, "I will see you at 4 o'clock".

"You didn't answer my question?"

I said, "I have an appointment but will be finished around 2 o'clock. See you later".

***

Outside a thick fog covered what felt like the whole world. On this foggy morning, I went to translate Roya's sad story for her doctor.

Finding the right treatment for Roya meant strangers – people from other religions and cultures, people who didn't even speak her own language - had to become familiar with all her sadness.

I put Roya's full story in front of her doctor, and he listened with amazement. He thought it was a tragedy, written by a skilled writer. After that, the doctor selected a day for visiting Roya in the following week. I made a note of the date and left the office.

I walked slowly along the pavement. My body was moving but my soul was sunk in Roya's destiny. Sometimes I brushed against others unconsciously, and had to make my apologies. Farhad's words kept repeating in my ears. Sometimes girls run from home and because of the fear of loss of reputation, they say she is dead.

I wanted to know more about the death of young Roya. This vague point was eating at my brain. Roya's destiny was a turning point for a new start. I bought a phone card from the store and returned home. I changed my clothes, took the phone and called my aunt in Herat.

"Hello, dear aunt."

"Hello, Homa dear. What has happened that you call your old aunt?"

"I'm always calling you, but this time I want to ask you about Roya."

"Roya? Who is Roya?"

Poor Roya, her name was erased from everyone's minds.

"Roya, daughter of Haj Rasoul who died at a young age."

"Ohh…" She said like her mind started working overtime.

"Now, why are you asking about her?"

"I want to know if she is really dead?"

"To tell you the truth, no."

"So where is she?"

"Nobody knows. in the Taliban era, she went missing on a visit with her mother to the cemetery. Her mother knew something, but she never revealed the secret."

"And why did they say she was dead?"

"Her father was a cruel and fanatical man, afraid of what people would say. Also, Roya was his step-daughter and there was no kindness there. First, he put his wife under a lot of pressure to reveal her location, and when she said nothing, he planned to pronounce her dead if anyone asked. Her mother was satisfied with that. I was sure she knew everything and had hatched this plan to release her daughter from the cruelty of her father and brothers. Roya didn't have a good life; many times, her father wanted to give her away. "

It seemed that thinking about the past was reflected for my dear aunt in the sadness of her voice as we continued talking.

"Well, is there anything else, aunt? My phone limit is coming to an end."

"No, my girl. When will you come to Herat? I want to see you while I am still alive."

"Soon, inshallah."

"I kiss your beautiful face from far away."

"I kiss your hands."

"Goodbye."

Both satisfaction and sorrow took my body. I felt weak, and I sank down on the couch. A thousand unanswered questions filled my mind; was my guess about Roya right, is she the lost Roya? She went away from her family because of the cruelty, and faced many difficulties. I should solve this mystery, but where to start? Who could I get to help me?

I was so taken up with my ideas that I didn't notice the passing of time until I heard the door key turning in the lock and realised it was gone 4 o'clock.

Farhad said, "hello".

I answered him reluctantly.

"Well, well, what a warm welcome for me," he said teasingly.

"Don't play with me, Farhad. I am not in the mood."

"Is there a problem?"

"I can't talk about it right now. I'm too upset."

Farhad changed his clothes and went to the kitchen. He made two cups of coffee and put them down on the table.

Then, as he picked up the phone he said, "what do you want to eat. today, be my guest."

"You order for me. I'll have whatever you're having."

After ordering the food, he sat beside me on the couch. He hugged me, and gently stroked my hair as he asked, "what has made my Homa sad? Have you been thinking about the past, again?"

His gentle words touched me, and perversely set my tears flowing again. I sobbed loudly as I told him Roya's story.

"And you think this is the Roya who was lost?"

"I don't think. I know. But I need the evidence."

"So, it is not sad; let's eat to power our brains and find a solution."

I wasn't hungry but didn't want to break his heart, so I ate to please him. We didn't talk; maybe like me he was thinking about how this would end.

I cleared the table and made two cups of tea, then I joined Farhad who was watching TV in the lounge.

He muted the TV and said, "I'm listening miss, you have my full attention."

I said, "I told you all the details; now it's your turn to find a solution."

He asked me, "when is the next meeting with Roya's doctor?"

"Next week."

"Then, next week you must tell the doctor all that you have told me. He will guide you according to the situation as he sees it."

After that, I found I could smile again, and I kissed his face.

***

It was nearly spring, but there was still no sign of it yet in this snow-covered city of Oslo. Here spring is slow to come and then disappears at the end of April, turning to cold, rainy days. I was heading slowly towards the hospital armed with a black umbrella and a scarf wrapped round me for warmth. I was concentrating on what I would I say to the doctor? What would he say to my request?

I heard a voice from other side of door, calling to get my attention, "dear Homa, dear Homa".

It was Vahid, Roya's son who was calling to me politely. On seeing him, I remembered his mother's story. This powerful youth was the result of his mother's hard struggles throughout the years.

"Hello."

"Hello Vahid, are you ok? How is your mother?"

"Nothing has changed. You read my mother's diary?"

"Yes, I read it."

"Is it useful for her treatment?"

"I don't know. You will have to ask her doctor."

A short time passed until it was our turn. The psychologist asked for me.

I entered the room. Roya was also there with the nurse. Her situation concerned me. Her dirty hair and clothes showed how deeply depressed she had become. It was like she couldn't see us. She walked right past us without paying us any attention, and sat in a corner. The Doctor said he was ready to begin.

"Roya, we read your diary. You write beautifully."

"Yes, I used to write a lot before."

"Why not now?"

She shrugged her shoulders, gave a harsh laugh and said, "what's the use?"

"I'm going to give you homework. I want you to write again, and then bring what you have written to me the next time you come to see me. Can you do that?"

"Maybe ..."

"As I understand it, after Saeid's death, you stopped writing?"

"He is not dead."

"So, write your memory of what happened after that little by little, as you wish. Promise me?"

"I'll try."

I translated their questions and answers for forty-five minutes, when Roya left, I asked the doctor to give me a few minutes of his time which he agreed to.

Without wasting time, he asked, "how can I help you?"

I said, "I read her diary and realized I know her."

He looked at me in amazement and emphasized, "you know her, how?"

"Yes, I know her family. Do you think her mental health is stable enough for me to be able to discuss this with her?"

"I don't know. I can't make that decision alone. There will have to be a meeting and I will discuss it with the other doctors. If your presence is necessary, I will call you. And you can't work as a translator in this case because of your personal relationship with her."

"That's okay. I know the rules very well. I just ask you to help me to find the truth."

"Sure, as long as it helps to treat Roya."

He followed me to the waiting room, where Vahid was still waiting there alone, and he invited him in.

Vahid was just going in when I called to him and said, "Vahid, I will wait for you outside".

He nodded his head briefly in acknowledgement and followed the therapist into this room.

The cold wind was blowing, chilling me to the very centre of my bones. I shrugged my shoulders, and thrust my hands deep into my pocket as I waited for Vahid on a wooden bench. In my mind I was rehearsing the best way to tell him the truth, when the sound of Vahid approaching put a stop to all that.

"Pardon me for keeping you waiting so long in this cold weather."

"Not, it's okay. would you like to walk?"

"Yes, that will be good."

As we walked along the path Vahid asked me if it was about his mother's illness that I wanted to talk.

I chose my words carefully. I told him that in reading her diary, I had realized that I almost certainly knew her family.

His eyes opened wide, "what?"

"Yes, your mother was our neighbour in Herat. You see, Vahid, many years ago a girl with the of name Roya was separated from family in Afghanistan for some reason. Now after reading her diary, I think your mother is that girl. I can't work as her translator any more according to the rules, since now it is a personal issue."

"I am very happy to find you, I think the main reason for her illness is how alone she is. Destiny has played strange games with her life. Now, after many years in this foreign country, with her in this critical condition, you are a valuable God-given gift. But please excuse me for now - I have a class at 12 o'clock."

"Vahid, I'd like you to come for lunch with me later, so we can get to know each other. I'll text you the address."

"No dear aunt … I won't bother you."

"Now you have called me aunt, you should definitely come to my home."

"So, I will come at 4 o'clock. Goodbye for now."

Vahid went to the bus station, and I continued on my way slowly.

***

The house was like a market in utter chaos. I dropped my clothes in one corner and went straight to the kitchen to prepare the food. I washed the rice and got some meat out of the fridge. Then I started cleaning. When the house was clean and tidy, I cooked Ghabeli. After finishing all my chores, I was just drinking some tea, when Farhad got home.

"Hello miss, you're back to your old self again?"

"Hello, yes, but change your clothes fast, we have a guest coming."

"I thought you prepared the food for me."

"How rude you are Farhad. Haven't I made enough for you as well?"

"I was kidding, Now who is yourguest?"

"Vahid."

"Vahid? Do I know him?"

"Roya's son. Now change your clothes. I'll tell you all about it later."

Farhad had just gone to change his clothes when the doorbell rang. I opened the door and there was Vahid, saying hello, and handing me a bunch of beautiful flowers.

"Hello my son. You are very welcome, but you didn't need to go through the bother of bringing me flowers?"

"Don't make me sorry, aunt."

I took the flowers, guided him into the lounge and invited him to sit down.

When Farhad entered, Vahid stood up, shook hands and introduced himself.

"I am Farhad, Homa's husband."

"Nice to meet you."

"I am very pleased to meet you, too."

Farhad turned to me and said, "I'm very hungry".

"Food is ready. Please come and sit at the table."

We ate the food with relish, and both men complimented me on my cooking. I cleared the table and joined them with tea. I sat beside Farhad and asked the younger man how long he had been living here.

"Only a year."

Farhad said, "are you on a language course?"

"No, I finished the language course, and now I am a student."

I said, "mashallah, it seems you are very talented."

Farhad asked, "what grade are you in?"

" Year eleven. I want to study law like my father, if God wills it. What is your expertise?"

Farhad said, "I am a final year student in journalism."

I said, "Vahid, don't be worried. Your path to progress is clear. If you work hard, you will get results."

"I hope so, too, but it is my mother who is my biggest concern now."

I said, "don't be worried, everything will be fine soon".

After we spent a lot of time talking, Vahid wanted to leave. We were sorry to see him go but escorted him politely to the door.

That night, laying warm and rested in the circle of Farhad's arms, I felt free from all concerns and soon we were making love.

***

I was sat in front of the TV watching the BBC, sunk deep in my own thoughts, idly playing with the remote. So many bad stories from my homeland distracted my daily activities. All these years away from Afghanistan, and not a second without concerns for my people. I suffered through my job, like I was at the heart of the problem. There was news from every corner: Herat, the land of flaming fires for women, Bamiyan, the land of blades, killing people because of their ethnicity and the northern cities where women were stoned for no reason …

That day, the bitter destiny of Roya was heavy on me. Even in the sad pictures showing on the TV, I saw her face, crying in the dirt in a corner. The sound of my mobile caught my attention - there was a message from Roya's doctor inviting me to attend a meeting with her and her colleagues. I went to Farhad's room filled with joy. He was confused by my abrupt entrance and stopped his work and came to me.

"What happened?"

"I received a message from Roya's doctor."

"Well?"

"They accepted my help."

Farhad was always looking for an opportunity to become closer to me, so this was a good time and he used it to hug me and then we went together into the lounge.

We sat on the couch, and he put his two hands on my shoulders and kissed my lips, saying, "don't forget your own Farhad with the coming of this new cousin?"

I said, "you're feeling jealous?"

As he got up and walked through to the kitchen he said, "what can I do? I won't share you with anyone."

"You never change."

He returned with two cups of tea, then said, "now come sit with your husband and make all his tiredness disappear. You know you don't ever want me to change".

Then I asked him about his work; "what are you working on now?

"I want to write an article about the laws on asylum. It's going to be a study about Afghans in European countries. And Homa, as you were a translator at the immigration office before, I was wondering if you can you help me?"

"I don't know any more than you, and even if I did know I wouldn't be allowed to talk to you about it. I can't reveal personal information because of the data protection laws.

"You would harm us with this sense of responsibility?"

"Dear Farhad, I swore an oath. Do you understand?"

"Okay, I surrender my lady."

I took a sip of my tea and said, "Farhad, how do you think this story will end?"

"It is clear, you will find this is a new cousin.

I was distracted by his words that hinted at the destiny of all Afghans, if they continued to escape from their country.

Farhad whispered painfully, "while there is war and blood, there will always be escape and homelessness. You know how many died on their way to Europe this year? Many drowned at sea and others were attacked by police in different countries. Human rights organizations don't care about it. Those who do manage to get to safety after many difficulties, then spend many years in undesirable camps. But a terror of being returned to Afghanistan makes them tremble with fear. Even if they aren't deported, this long wait makes them depressed and sick."

I said, "our people are being punished for the inefficiency and corruption of successive Afghan governments. If they just thought a little about their people instead of making money, it would not be so bad.

There's such a huge societal gap in Afghanistan and by increasing the value of the bank accounts of the rich, the poor people of Kabul became weaker each day."

"That is so true."

I enjoyed talking to Farhad. He is a wise and hardworking man who is also very knowledgeable. In these years since we had left our own country, he had studied hard and soon he would become an active journalist. We were awake until midnight and talked about many things. We went to bed, tired of the pains of these people. In hope of tomorrow, we closed our eyes.

***

I was nervous about all the many experts who would be sitting around the long table at this meeting. I entered the room timidly and shook hands with many of the members, introduced myself and then sat beside Ms Olsen who I knew from before. The head of the therapy center began the discussion.

"You claim you know Roya, and want to take part in her treatment?"

"Yes."

We are here to discuss this issue today so we can reach the desired outcome."

Ms Olsen was writing something on the paper in front of her and said, "I think the presence of Homa will have a positive impact on Roya's treatment. Roya should sign a consent form, so we make you aware of her secrets."

The chief indicated his approval by nodding his head and said, "I agree with you".

I had only been listening up until then, but now cut in with, "but I understand there is a law which allows the patient's relatives to sign on their behalf if they have difficulties with decision making; for example Vahid, Roya's son, could sign instead of her ".

"Yes there is such law, but not for patients like Roya. It is just for patients who don't have the mental capacity for decision making. They don't have a healthy brain. Roya has the power of recognition. It's just that she has a very deep depression."

Ms Olsen continued, "anyway rightly or wrongly, we should tell her the realities. Secondly, I don't think this shock will be bad for her".

The doctor in charge of the discussion said, "I agree with Ms Olsen".

He summed up, "so the majority vote is to talk with Roya about this situation. Then he looked at me and said, "we will inform you if you are required".

When the meeting ended, I went home. I was fighting within myself and wondered for how much long they would discuss it?

Norway's system is very bureaucratic. For a simple case, you would have to take several different letters and be present in many meetings. For people coming from Asian countries, this much paperwork is a little difficult. We can't cope with all the paperwork. The meeting on that day was rather too much for me. Since it took the only free time in my schedule, I would have to hurry to get there in time for my next translation.

It was 4 o'clock by the time I reached home. As always, I emptied the mailbox and took the letters and ads with me. I was tired from all the discussions that day; the Roya meeting and the translation work at the immigration office were circling around in my head. I couldn't concentrate. Without paying any attention to the chaos the house was in I went directly to the bedroom. It was like I needed eternal relaxation. Because of the tiredness, I just dropped the letters from my hand, sank down on the bed and knew nothing then until I was awoken with the gentle touch of a hand on my head.

"Homa, Homa."

I opened my eyes, stretched and said hello.

Farhad smiled and said, "I came home to eat lunch with you, but now we should eat dinner together".

I looked out the window. It was dark outside. I said that I was sorry, I was very tired.

He offered his hand towards me. I took it and he pulled me up. Chaos no longer reigned in the house and the aroma of fried chicken permeated the air.

I turned to Farhad and said, "thank you, you've gone through a lot of trouble for me. I'll take a bath and make a cup of tea for us to drink together."

"okay, but be quick since we have guests coming."

I wondered, and said, "guests? Without me being informed? Farhad, I've told you before many times…

I hadn't finished speaking but he interrupted saying, "take a bath now. When you see the guests, you will kiss me instead of fighting".

The hot water removed all my tiredness, and I became happy again. In the mirror, I enjoyed watching my beautiful body and long hair. I thought to myself, I am still young and beautiful, and smiled with satisfaction. I put on a short robe with a pattern of small black flowers. It suited me well and I felt a hundred times more beautiful.

As I was just applying some pink lipstick, Farhad knocked on the door and said, "come out, our guests have arrived".

I went out anxiously. I couldn't say anything. Roya and Vahid! Roya should be at the hospital; what was she doing here?

I went towards them, as they both stood up out of respect. I hugged and kissed Roya. She had the smell of familiarity and closeness. I shook hands with Vahid and then sat beside my husband.

I asked Roya, "are you better?"

Thank God, still breathing. Vahid has taken a week off work and has brought me home. Tonight, we have come to bother you".

"You aren't any bother?"

I made some excuse to go and see Farhad who was cooking in the kitchen.

I said to Farhad, "what is this game you are playing?"

"How is it anything to do with me? Ask Vahid."

My mind was troubled. I crept quietly to the bedroom, took my mobile and rang Vahid's number.

"Hello."

"Hello Vahid. Can you leave your mother for a moment and go into the other room so we can speak easier."

After a few seconds he said, "okay. I'm out of the room, what's the matter?"

" I didn't know you were coming tonight. What is this about?"

"Actually, the doctor has released my mother into my care and said that if we had any problems, to contact the hospital. I brought her here tonight to discuss the matter with her as a first step.

"So, you made the effort and brought her here tonight to introduce us. Ican see how she is and talk to her slowly. Now go back to your mother. I'll be with you in a moment."

I hung up and joined the guests. Roya was clean and tidy now and had a tiny smile on her lips. She was wearing a navy-blue shirt and her skin looked brighter than usual. She wore a ring with a beautiful gem on her frail-looking hand. I thought to myself maybe this is the valuable ring that Roya's mother sent to her as a sign when she was in Iran.

I started talking and said, "I was tired today and slept when I got home. Farhad was kind and didn't wake me up. Tonight, we eat the food made by a restaurant chef. I will make some salad while you talk and set the table."

Roya said," I will help," and she followed me into the kitchen.

While I was making the salad, I turned to Roya and said, "you are really beautiful".

She put the plates on the table slowly and said, "I like writing very much, but when God took my most valuable things, I returned this ability to him, too".

"Don't give up hope. God gave you a big asset when he gave you Vahid."

"Of course, having Vahid is a blessing, but you would give me the right to complain, if you knew how difficult it was protecting him."

"Did you start writing that day you promised the doctor you would begin again?"

"No, I'm not interested in taking up my pen again. In fact, the pen and paper won't accept me."

"Practice - your ability will return for sure."

The table was set, everything was ready, and I invited everyone to come and sit down. There was a warm atmosphere which I had not experienced in a long time. Everyone was enjoying the party. Even Roya, who was suffering with depression, had a smile on her lips.

Later Farhad took the guests home while I cleared everything up and thought about the best way to talk with Roya. I was in a hurry to embrace her like an old relative, after years of desperation.

When Farhad returned, I thanked him for that night. I went to him, put my hands around his back and my lips close to him, I could smell his warm and desirable breath.

"Thanks for everything, you are a good husband."

"Well, do you want to reward me?"

"What do you want?"

When you have finished, I shall be in our bedroom to collect my reward.

I smiled and said, "really? I never know when you are serious or not".

He said, "I am serious now", and went towards the bathroom.

I cleaned everything, got my work things and my clothes ready for the morning and then slept with love next to my husband.

***

It was the middle of march and near the time of the new solar year. The grass was growing. On that clear and sunny Saturday, I had a chance to introduce Roya to Norway's environment. I wanted Farhad to take this day off work so we could go to the coast. The cries of the birds were mixed with the sound of the waves, and a golden ray of sunshine, which is a rare blessing here, shone down in all its beauty. Dressed in a brown coat with stripes and a silk scarf Roya looked like an attractive and adorable woman.

I said, "you have very good style, sister".

"Sister … I had sisters."

"I read it in your diary."

"But I have had no news of them for years."

"I wish you were the same Roya."

She asked with curiosity, "which Roya?"

I was worried that maybe she would feel bad and changed the subject saying, "anyway have you ever been to the beach before?"

"No, but my life was full of waves and these waves here are nothing compared to them."

Roya enjoyed watching the sea and was so taken up with it that she didn't say much. Maybe because I talk a lot myself, that is why I expected her to do so, too.

When some dark clouds came and hid the sun, I took Roya to an Iranian restaurant. She ate very politely. Poverty hadn't destroyed her culture.

This time she started the conversation, saying, "please talk about this Roya". I didn't expect this question and stopped for a few seconds.

"Roya, the girl who lived on other side of the fig river."

She dropped her glass and made her scarf all wet. She started firing questions at me. "Name of mother? Father? Grandfather?"

I answered these questions as best I could one at a time.

I could almost hear her heart thumping in her chest, she was so shocked. There were tears in her eyes and she looked at me closely. She stood up slowly, her hand on the table for support. She came towards me slowly. I waited for a hug or maybe cries of joy. But she looked at me in disbelief - she said she didn't believe it.

I said she'd be better not to say anything now, we could talk later. I took her shoulders and after paying the bill, moved to the vehicle parked beside the restaurant.

We drove towards the house. It was nearly sunset. I asked Farhad for some help and sent Roya to the bedroom.

I hadn't seen anyone in this condition before. It was very strange. Her eyes were open wide, but she didn't say anything or move. It was like she was sleeping with her open eyes. I left the room quietly, called Vahid and talked to him.

He said, "aunt, please leave my mother alone until I come and don't talk to her."

"Sure, my son. But come quickly. You know her illness and will be of more use than me".

"I'm on my way now."

He arrived about an hour later and rushed to her side directly.

"Hello mother."

"You've come, my son? I thought it was Homa. It is not safe for us here. We should go, she will inform Hadji Rasoul."

Vahid stopped her and said, "you are in shock. You remember what the doctor said? Don't try to talk while you are like this. Just take your medicine and sleep."

He turned to me and said, "aunt, please bring a glass of water".

I got it for him quickly. He took the pill out of his pocket and gave it to his mother with the water. Roya sat up with difficulty, swallowed the pill and then slept again.

Vahid said gently, "now we leave you alone to rest".

Roya nodded her head and closed her eyes.

We both left the room. She was alone with her pain.

Vahid said, "sorry aunt, her fear of the past is with her always. She thinks they still follow her; it is all in her imagination".

I said I understood.

***

I turned the door handle slowly and entered the room. Vahid was sitting on the floor resting his head next to his mother's side. She was asleep. Tears came to my eyes; it was beautiful to see the attachment this young man had for his mother. I put my hand on his shoulder.

He opened his eyes and said quickly, "it's you?"

I said, "get up my son, you must use the bed I made up for you, otherwise you will suffer with your back tomorrow".

He thanked me. I said goodbye and left the room. Their loneliness was on my mind. I was awake for hours.

***

In the morning I opened my eyes at the sound of migrating birds on this beautiful Norwegian spring day. I got washed and dressed. I laid the breakfast table ready. After waking Farhad, I went to the guest bedroom where Roya and Vahid were still peacefully sleeping. I woke up Vahid gently and said, "it's time to get up son, it's 10 o'clock.

"Hello, good morning."

"Good morning to you. Is it okay to wake her up, do you think?

"You go, my mother and I will come, too."

I said, "okay" and left the room.

I found myself staring at the bubbles on the surface of the hot milk. I stopped and added the cinnamon to it. But then I froze as I saw the pain that Roya was suffering. The dark circles under her eyes were deeper and more worried than ever. For a moment I regretted what I had done yesterday. And wished that I hadn't shared the truth with her. The doctor had told me that if anyone mentioned about safety and the end of her escape, her anxiety levels increased.

Vahid interrupted my thoughts as he said 'hello'. The cinnamon had spilled from the spoon and was like dust on the front of my white shirt.

Farhad said, "are you all right". Go change your shirt, I will finish getting the milk ready".

After I had shed many tears, I changed my shirt and returned to the kitchen. I went directly to Roya. I kissed her cheek and asked if she felt any better.

she said, "I am okay. And now, by finding you, I am better".

I sat beside her and said, "I am happy, but we better not talk about it".

Roya was putting butter on her bread and said, "I have many questions to ask."

Vahid answered instead of me and said mother, "you've been told lots of times that stress is poison for you".

I added, "you'll get all the answers you want, but at the right time".

After eating breakfast, I was clearing the table when Vahid came close and said, "aunt if you will allow it, we will leave now".

With a heavy heart I asked him why.

He said his mother needed rest and by staying here, her memories were coming back to trouble her.

***

Roya was sometimes at home and sometimes at the hospital. Her situation changed frequently. Some days she was very happy without any signs of illness, and other days she was very ill.

Around 11o'clock, my phone pinged. It was a message from Farhad reminding me not to forget Roya's birthday. Time was passing slowly. I spent more time looking at the clock than doing my job that day. It made me crazy. At exactly 4 o'clock, I collected my things and left. Unluckily for me the lift was out of order and had still not been repaired. I had to find the energy to run down five flights of stairs, which somewhat delayed me. I could see the lights of Farhad's silver motor blinking from afar. I hurried as quickly as I could to end his wait.

"Hello dear."

"Hello lady."

"Where are we going?"

"First, the flower shop and then the confectionary shop to make a surprise for Roya and Vahid."

Roya was having one of her better days, and she let me give her a hug and call her sister. We sat together and talked.

While she was opening the box with our gifts I said, "it was a big day for me when I found my Roya after so many years".

Roya seemed inspired. She wasn't shocked. While putting the flowers in a crystal pot she said, "today is the death of my loneliness, finding you ends many years of emptiness".

I went to her and hugged her. The tears then slid down her cheeks and we cried together.

After we were done with crying, I said, "be calm, my dear sister. We are happy today".

I took her by the shoulder and guided her to a seat. Vahid and Farhad watched with silent joy, not wanting to break in on this moment we shared together.

I was with Roya that night and we talked a lot. She had many questions, I had the answers for her. Her first question was 'where is my mother'.

I said, "my dear, you lost her many years ago."

Her shoulders shook and she said, "how did she die?"

I don't remember much but as I was told, during the Taliban era, your father and brother were accused of spying and executed. The difficulty of life made your mother ill, and she died before your sisters Parvin and Pouran were fully grown. With the hard work your mother put in and the wealth of Hadji Rasoul, your sisters grew up. At the end of the Taliban era, schools opened, and the sisters studied. When I was in eighth grade, your mother became seriously ill and died a year later. After her death, Parvin and Pouran were alone, and an aunt took them in. About a year later they were both married. Pouran and her husband, Ahmad, still live in her father's house.

Roya listened carefully and after I had finished whispered, "I would give all my life if I could just once more rest my head on my mother's knees or reach out my hand and stroke her hair.

I wiped the tears from my eyes and said, "I am alone too. You are like a mother for me, and I for you. Roya, you escaped, and no one is following you anymore, no one is coming to kill you. I will soon find a phone number for your sisters, and then we will go to visit them in Herat. The doctor said it would be safe to travel to see your family; you will be fine. But now it is your turn to continue your story after the death of Saeid."

She said, "I am with you tonight and I know your curiosity will keep you awake unless I tell you my story. I will tell you of the pain I have carried in my chest for many years."

I put my head on her knees, and she stroked my hair like a mother who wanted to tell her daughter a story. It was a good feeling; nobody had touched me like that for years. It was like being in the arms of a mother ...

She started her story like this;

Chapter 9

After the death of Saeid, my whole world was devasted. All roads for me were at a dead end. I was alone with a fatherless child and my father and mother-in-law was broken by this. The fortieth day after Saeid's death, father called me. All the family were gathered. I sat beside them and listened.

Father touched my head and said, "you are my daughter, and I don't want you to suffer anymore. Now I say you are free to marry anyone; me and Saeid's mother will support and help you.

I said, "I didn't expect that from you, father; Is that really your idea of my personality?"

Mother said with a shaken and painful sound, "girl we are old and will die soon, and then you and Vahid will need someone to support you. On the other hand, you are an adult, and free to decide for yourself".

I said, "thank you but I have made my decision. The rest of my life will be centered entirely around Vahid. Like the past was full of Saeid. And I want your help to do this".

All the members of the family kissed me and offered their support.

I cried with them, and when that long night had finally turned into morning, I left them and went to my lonely room. From that day I swore to Saeid's spirit that I would become strong enough to overcome my problems to raise our child.

***

By the start of the month of mehr (the seventh month of the Solar Hijri calendar), I sent Vahid to school and put flowers in the empty place that should have been Saeid's. Father took the hand of his grandchild and took him for his first day of school.

After Vahid left, I took the phone book and went to the market. The sun was still shining in this world without Saeid, and people and life were carrying on without him. The phone box was busy as always. When it was my turn, I took the phone book and called all my relatives. I told them that if they heard of a job for a woman, to call me. I walked slowly along the pavement and looked idly at the colourful shops. Then I spotted an ad in the window of the vegetable store - 'We need workers for washing vegetables."

I went inside quickly. A fat man dressed in green asked me what I wanted

"I've come in answer to this ad in the window."

"Can you take 10 kilos of vegetables and wash them for practice today? But since I don't know you, please pay for it first."

"Okay. Thank you."

The man weighed the vegetables. Then I thought to myself, 'Roya you don't have the money to pay for them'. I looked at my fingers - the wedding ring that Saeid had given me and the one from my mother. I should give one of them to pay for the vegetables. I couldn't betray Saeid's memory, so I used my mother's ring. It was very valuable, but I took it from my finger and gave it to him and asked him if he would accept the ring as a deposit for the vegetables.

He said, 'no problem' and he took the ring and gave me the vegetables.

By the time Vahid had come home from his first day at school, I had started what proved to be a hard job. Father was a little sad, but I told him that I didn't want to be a burden to him and he accepted that.

I said to him, "I am young and can work".

***

One morning when the weather was dark and cloudy like a venom on my old scars, I put a pack of cleaned vegetables in front of the store.

Mr Abbas looked at them and said, "hello, Ms Roya".

I said, "hello brother, please take these vegetables and pay me what you owe me up until today as I need the money for my son's school".

While opening the till he said, "time passes so quickly. It seems like just yesterday that you came for a job, and already a year has passed".

I preferred to keep my silence when answering men, as I was not able to be careless. While I stood there quietly, he continued, "Ms Roya in this last year I have seen many bad things with my eyes, but not from you".

"Thanks brother."

"Look at yourself? More broken than last year. I don't want bad things for you. You deserve better. I have a daughter, and you a son. We're both single, be a nice woman and accept my proposal."

I wouldn't listen to it and said, "what is my account Mr Abbas? And please can you return the ring".

"Which ring?"

"The ring of my dead mother, the one I gave to you as a deposit for the vegetables."

"It is at home. Come tomorrow to collect it."

He put a pack of money in front of me and said, this is your year's salary, fully paid".

I took money and got out quickly. All the way home I could hear his words repeating repeatedly in my head and I was crying at the same time. God what should I do? Did he think that just because I am single, I am just waiting for a proposal?

Life was like a cup of poison, to be drunk slowly and kill you. On the one hand I had the pressure of the job and the need to pay for Vahid's schooling, and on other hand I had to put up with this sort of talk from people. It was making me tired. Sometimes I wished to go to an empty place and never see any Muslim people, every again. Mr Abbas proposed to me many times after that and each time I gave him a negative answer. But he would not let me alone; he was axe grinding on my soul. I decided to pay the money required for registering Vahid and then look for a new job. Only then could I be released from Mr Abbas. Drowning in my miseries, I found myself sadly waiting in the queue at the back of Vahid's school office.

I waited for hours for it to be my turn. I slowly become tired and sat down on the ground until one of the staff announced, "Afghans leave and come back on October 1st. There will be no registration for you this year until the new rules come in.

I left the office, feeling desperate, and went home. I was frantically thinking to myself what I could possibly tell Vahid? Surely, he would want to know about his registration. I decided to give an excuse and so escape having to explain everything about the problems of immigrants in society.

***

Father was sick for many months. His only hobby was talking with Vahid about his childhood memories. Vahid listened to what father said, anything from paper games to punishments in the home schools of Herat. He talked to his grandchild about everything from those days. He believed we shouldn't forget our origins just because of our migration. We might fall from the horse, but not from the source.

When I came home Vahid was eagerly listening to his grandfather's stories. But he left him and came rushing over when he saw me.

He said, "what happened mother? Did you enroll me to the school?"

I said, "no my son, I didn't have time today, but you are a smart student, maybe they will sign you up automatically". Father called Vahid back and I was released from his questions.

Tears slid down my face, But I pressed my cheeks hard to try and stop the flow. Because of all the vegetable cleaning, my hands were sore and worn. Signs of my destiny even at my young age were noticeable in my hands. They had become green. I studied my reflection in the mirror. Mr Abbas from the vegetableshop was right. I did look even more broken than the previous year. Without paying any attention to such sad thoughts, I washed my face and went to the kitchen to help mother.

"Hello."

"Hello my girl, you came?"

"Yes, I came to help you."

"The food is ready. Please put it on the table."

"Dear mother …"

"Yes, my dear …"

"Can you go to the vegetable shop tomorrow? To get back the ring I put as a deposit."

"Why don't you go yourself?"

"I have work to do."

"Okay, I will go. Shall I get the vegetables?"

No, I've got my salary; just recover the memorial ring my mother gave to me."

She asked with wonder, "why?"

"I'm tired of this job. I'm looking for another one."

"Well, you know best."

***

It was funny that God always showed the correct path as being easy. He never left me alone. Always big miseries and small chances came to me. Me and my child always had to work hard to stay alive, and not die from hunger.

It was one of those autumn days when the leaves were dropping from the trees, that Arezoo and her family came to visit father. When I saw Arezoo, I put my head on her heart, to hear Saeid's heart beating. That beloved heart given to the beautiful Gandhari girl.

That day when we talked about a job, Arezoo's father invited me to work at his embroidery workshop. It was a damaged and non-residential building in a suburb of the city. I had to wake up at 6:00 am to get there on time. As I waited for the bus, I could smell the unpleasant aroma of sweat in the crowd. At nights, in the darkness, I was imprisoned in my humane loneliness. I asked God about a thousand times for death, because of the humiliation and shame I was forced to experience.

I learned how to embroider completely within three months. It was a good job, but because of the long journey it made me very tired. I saw Vahid less and was careless about the education of my child.

***

The white tailored clothes were folded one by one, finished from unfinished ones in separate piles. Arezoo's father looked at me and said, "you can go dear Roya, and come back for more work on Saturday".

"If you will allow it, I could take some work home with me and do it on Friday."

"Okay, take them."

I carried them in a bag under my arm. I put my old veil over them. After saying goodbye, I exited through the big steel door of the workshop.

Snow laying on the ground everywhere, a white but clear sky made it possible to see the blessing of the moon. It was for me, a lonely road. Vehicles passed. I waited a few hours; my fingers went numb with the cold, until the light of a lamp from far away brought me to the road. A personal vehicle stopped beside me.

A voice asked, "where are you going, sister?"

I had my doubts as to whether to get in or not. The driver looked like a nice person, with wide shoulders and a long and clean beard. I told myself if I didn't get in, it was uncertain when another vehicle would come along. Interrupting my thoughts the driver repeated, "where to, sister?"

Stuttering with fear and the cold I said, "I'd appreciate it if you'll take me to the city zone".

He said, "get in please".

I opened the back door of vehicle and got in. I looked in the mirror and saw the driver studying me. I was a little afraid but tried to look relaxed.

He asked quickly, "what are you doing on road at this time of night?"

"I'm going home from work."

"Well, "what are you hiding under your veil?"

Fear seized me and my hands were shaking, but I tried to calm myself.

I said, "are you a driver or policeman?"

He said, "I am an officer who fights against drugs. From your accent I know you are Afghan. For how long are you going to make junkies out of the youth of this country?"

I couldn't tolerate anymore. I cried, but put the bag on the front seat of the vehicle and said, "take it and see how many kilos of drugs this poor woman has."

As he drove, he opened it up and saw the half-made embroidery work. Then he focused on my face through the mirror and apologized, "it is my job to question everyone".

I said, "stop, I want to get out".

He said, "I really am sorry. Give me your address, and I will take you home."

I said, "the fear in me doesn't end with one apology. I leave you to the God you talk about". Then I hit the window and said angrily, "stop".

The man become nervous then and stopped by the road. I dropped a 500 toman bill on the seat next to him and closed the bag and then sat beside that long road until I felt better. I was close to the city now, so I took the first taxi to get home.

After this happened, I was very ill. When father heard about it, he phoned Arezoo's father straight away to excuse me from work.

***

That cold afternoon, I hugged Vahid tightly to me and counted the lily flowers on the white cotton sheets. My son's eyes were closed, and I listened to the sound of his warm breath. My thoughts were awake and remembered the flames of Saeid's kisses. The fountain … me and Saeid. Safe, hugs and warm kisses… I wish this dream would never end. I wish I was sunk in the contentment of Saeid's kisses, and never had to face the typhoon.

The truth was that thinking about Saeid, kept me moving forward. Otherwise, I had no will of my own to go on.

The sound of mother's voice aroused me from my thoughts. I knew that the tears had wetted my face. I wiped them quickly away with the sleeve of my blue coat. I got up and went to answer her. I didn't want her calling me any louder and waking Vahid up from his sweet afternoon sleep.

"Yes, dear mother, do you have job for me to do?"

"Come my girl, we have guests."

I put on my clean lemon scarf. The one that looked beautiful on my white skin. And went to the living room. Arezoo, the new owner of Saeid's kind heart had come with her family to visit me again. When I walked in the room, they all stood up in respect to me. I hugged Arezoo and her mother, and talked with her father.

He said, "I know what happened to you and you are right not to come to work in the workshop. But there is another way you can continue your work".

I said, "what way?"

He said, "come with me".

We all went outside to the yard with him. In the corner there was an expensive sewing machine with all the tools necessary for embroidering. I was amazed and couldn't speak because of my happiness. I kept my calm and thanked him politely. I saw great pleasure in the eyes of mother and father.

I asked, "is this for the work I bring home to do?"

He stopped me and said, "you don't need to come. I will come every week, take away with me the work you have done and bring new work for you to do".

It was like a heavy weight was being lifted off my shoulders. I thanked him very much.

Arezoo hugged me and said, "you are a strong woman, I want to become just like you".

Tears wet the corner of my eye and I said, "be like me, but have a different destiny, not a dark one like mine".

That day when the family left, we emptied the outhouse that stood in the backyard with help of mother. It was good place for my small embroidery workshop.

On a cold Friday, Lina and Samei came to help me. Samei painted the walls and joked with Lina. I saw the beauty of their relationship, and remembered the old days with Saeid. It warmed my soul. My love and I; his presence making me feel content. The room was filled with lovely music. I put my head gently on his chest and his hand smoothed my long, wavy hair. I looked at him innocently.

"Saeid?"

"Yes."

"Never leave me alone."

"Are you crazy? Of course, we will be together always. One day we call to each other with old and tired voices. We will help each other for many years and even when we are old, we will be together."

Saeid couldn't keep his promise and left me in loneliness with a lot of problems. Samei's voice brought me out of my daydream.

"Dear Roya, dear Roya."

"Yes, yes."

"I've finished the painting. Leave the door of the workshop open tonight so the smell of paint will go away. You can bring your tools in tomorrow."

"Thank you for all your hard work."

Lina answered instead of Samei, "there's no need for thanks, it was nothing".

***

I stared at the beautiful embroidery frame mounted on the wall. The sound of Ahmad Zahir's music filled the workshop.

'*You came again my dear, people victims for you*
Me and a hundred like me, sincere to you, to you.'

I had a lot of memories associated to this song. Nights at the hospital at Herat. My burned heart and the beautiful voice of Saeid like water poured on the fire of desperation.

The seclusion and solitude of my small embroidery workshop took me back to the past, I stabbed my finger with the needle instead of the material many times. But I preferred this silence to the busy workshop of Arezoo's father. I escaped the inquisitive stares of people. What place could be better than here? I worked until late at night. Sometimes Vahid came with notes and lessons, after he had finally been allowed back to school, and we worked on the words. Hours, days and weeks passed, and I saw the results of my efforts over many years. My son grew every day, and he came to understand my problems better and tried to help me. Sometimes he worked with me in the workshop, that was more hopeful for me.

Vahid was raised in such a way that he learned that all problems were solvable for him. When I was sunk in economic problems, he worked for me. Unfortunately, one autumn day, when Vahid was thirteen, dear father passed away.

Yes, that day, Hadji Zabih, after a lot of problems and difficulties, left the family. I lost a big supporter and Vahid was deeply disturbed. I didn't know how to calm Lina and mother, or halt my son's tears. What would we do now without our caretaker?

When Hadji Zabih died, the love of his life, Faezeh, couldn't bear it for more than three months, before she, too, died. The loss of both father and mother broke my back. It was me and my teenage boy and a world of tears and regret.

Chapter 10

My head was on fire. I didn't know what I wanted from this world anymore. I got home feeling sick and tired. I reached inside my bag for the key. It wasn't a bag; it was a warehouse filled with clutter. I scrabbled amongst the contents searching inside my bag, when a hand reached over and touched my shoulder - it was Vahid.

"What are you looking for my dear mother?"

"I can't find the key."

He put his hand in the bag, finding it instantly and opened the door.

The same house, where I said goodbye to all my happiness. The house that the landlord was now insisting we vacate as he wanted to sell it.

He said, "did you have any luck today?"

I said "I searched all the real estates in the neighbourhood, and after a lot of problems and showing my id card and so on, they showed me some run-down houses that they want very high rents for. I will go again in the morning to see what can be done".

A huge amount of dust had entered my socks and their colour had changed. While taking them off, I said, "I did find some small places. We will go in the morning together to look at them".

At that point I realised that my sock was stuck to a bloody abscess that had formed on my leg. I quickly hid the sock and got up so Vahid wouldn't see my tears. In those days I hated life, Vahid was my only connection to it.

After a great deal of trouble and a lot of misery, we managed to find a small house to rent. But the nightmares wouldn't leave me alone at night, and my days were full of stress. I was forced to go to a psychiatrist. Within a few months our home became like a pharmacy and Vahid was my personal nurse. I tried so hard to keep healthy for Vahid's sake, but it was not possible. Everyone I saw gave me advice. I just wanted to yell at them to stop, I'd heard all this before. If you had a destiny like mine, you'd be dead instead of laying on this bed like me.

There were no jobs to be had. Our savings slowly drained away. Money for medicine and doctors were another problem.

One day when Arezoo and her family came to visit me, her father looked at me and said with satisfaction, "mashallah (this is what God wills), dear Vahid has grown, he will take your place in the workshop in one week".

I said in a shocked voice, "what? Vahid go to work in the workshop?"

He said, "yes, didn't you know?"

I called Vahid angrily.

"Yes dear mother."

"You haven't been going to school in the mornings?"

He bowed his head and said, "not from the day you became ill".

My world became darker than before. I said to myself, 'you did your job well Roya!'

But I said nothing out loud. When our guests had left, I sat Vahid beside me and asked him not to leave school. I said, "I promised your father".

I got up with enormous difficulty in the morning, And I went to the school with my boy and explained the reason for his absence to the head teacher.

I returned home happy but weak. When I entered the alley where I live, I saw Lina and Samei waiting for me. I unlocked the door and opened it as I greeted them, and we went inside together.

Lina said, "you are tired. Sit down, and I will make some tea".

I asked Samei about their family and Lina raised her voice from the kitchen and asked where Vahid was? I cried as I told her the story of his not going to school and said, "see I am useless? I haven't kept the promise I gave to his father".

Lina kissed me and said, "you will get well soon. It is a minor illness caused by loneliness".

Samei stopped her and said, "one of our relatives flew to Europe for treatment yesterday. Why don't you apply, too?"

I said, "you have great ideas, but I don't have an incurable illness to be sent to Europe. It is simply depression that I am suffering from".

Samei said, "you have no one to take care of you and you need help. Don't interfere; give me your documents and I will make the request and send it to the United Nations office".

I said reluctantly, "okay, but how could I ever adapt to Europe? I would lose the few people that I have left here, too".

Lina said, "you should try because of Vahid's future".

When it was about Vahid, I lost the power to fight. I got up, got my documents and gave them to Samei. I talked to Lina a lot then, speaking of the past and the sadness I had inside me.

As Samei was leaving, I saw him slip his hand under blanket we had been sitting on. I knew what he had done and become worried. I said nothing because I needed that money. My women's honour was touched. I accepted this being forced on me because of my child and thanked Lina and told her this was only a loan, and that I would pay her back.

The antidepressants I was taking made me heavy. Waking every morning was like rising from the dead. I got up with difficulty and said goodbye to Vahid. I didn't want him missing school and becoming sad and depressed because of my illness.

Every few months, the number of pills I had to take was increased. I was a living corpse. I had two open eyes, that followed Vahid's steps. My world had become the four walls of my room, and I lay on my bed day and night. My home was like small pharmacy with shelves full of anti-depression pills. My days were dark and nights even darker. A year had passed from the start of my illness and not much had changed since then.

I existed in a world of pain spent thinking about the past, reviewed old albums and old memories in my mind. I helped Vahid with his schoolwork. I breathed with his ideas, which were full of hope.

The winter of that year was sad. Vahid's head was in his books in one corner, and I lay stinking in my bed. We were both in mental breakdown. I kept telling Lina not to leave Vahid alone, and she was very kind to him. She usually came on Fridays. She would clean the house and then take Vahid to go and have fun with her family.

On one of these Fridays Samei had news of our asylum application. We were accepted in one of the countries in northern Europe. Vahid was very excited on hearing this news. But my smile was short-lived. I didn't know what to do. If we were alone in a foreign land, what would happen to us? We were told that we should be ready for to leave in the spring. My own happiness was buried in illness, but Vahid's happiness gave me strength.

The engraved words on Saeid's tombstone were full of dust. It looked like nobody had visited during the winter. I cleaned it with the blue cotton cloth I had brought from home and sat on his tomb.

'Hello my Saeid. I have come to say goodbye to your cold tomb. Me and our beloved son are going away to a far country. Even more foreign than here. This weak body will remain alive until she has finished her objective.

Vahid cried and placed the yellow flowers we had brought with us over the tomb.

I put my hand on his head and said, "enough, get up now and we will go".

His beautiful eyes were red from crying, but he hid his sadness for a second. I could remember crying when my own father died. It was like my destiny was being repeated for my son. Without caring for these ideas, we left the graveyard.

In the last week, we gave our home back to the owner who was a kind man. We stayed those last few days at Lina's house. We laughed in the evenings talking over our shared memories. Sometimes we cried. On the last day, all our life of poverty was packed into two small boxes. It was just like the time when we entered Iran. The difference was that back then I had the kind hands of Saeid and mother and father to help me.

It was time to say goodbye to our only supporter in Iran. I hugged Lina for the last time and talked to all the members of her family. I had a feeling that I would never see them again, just like my mother and sisters back in Afghanistan.

Vahid and I were both still sobbing as we passed down the corridor that led to the plane. We sat on our seats. We felt a strange lack of safety. I grabbed Vahid's hand. Where would this migration end? Norway was our destination… where was that? What would the people be like? We had many unanswered questions.

We arrived in what felt like another world – I could hardly believe it. Two beautiful women and one man came to welcome us. One was from our country and translated our words and that silenced my pains. It was a small town in the south of Norway, beautiful with a wild but lively environment. It was almost poetic, but very unfamiliar.

I sat looking out of the windows for hours. The strangest thing for me, was when I couldn't contact others. By winter, the city was completely clothed in white.

You know the rest. The same psychologist and repeated words. Walking every day and seeing unknown people with cold shoulders moving quickly.

I came to love my bed and never wanted to leave it. It was like death to me. And Vahid was imprisoned there with me. I was angry. Eventually we were forced to move to Oslo, the capital and here you see us dear Homa, and I am with you today.

***

It was morning and we were both very tired with bleary eyes still leaking tears. We looked at each other and I was still sunk in the intricacies of Roya's story. I leaned my head on her shoulder, and she gently stroked my hair.

***

When summer came, everyone was a lot more content and beautiful smiles started to appear on people's faces. We were going to forget about the frozen winter with its feeble, watery kind of sunshine. I was given permission to visit Roya more often. The doctor believed that my role in her treatment was critical. In cases of extreme depression, it is not known how patients will react in different scenarios, so she didn't have permission to travel to Afghanistan. Her mind was full of waves like the sea. Multiple attempts at suicide were documented and it worried me. I preferred her to be kept in bed. But Vahid's sadness couldn't be ignored. Vahid asked the doctor to let them spend the summer together. She agreed.

Usually, we spent two to three days together. On good days I didn't want them to end. In the spring I always suffered from hay fever. I always seemed to be tired. I would sit in front of the TV with a tissue ready for the coughs and sneezes on one side and my decongestant spray on the other. Basically, I couldn't do very much at all. Farhad ordered food for us but

God brought me Roya, my angel of kindness. She put the plate of soup on the table in front of me and ordered me to eat it.

"It is good for you", she would say.

I took her hand and said, "sister, sit beside me". She would gently put her kind hand on my head and say again, "eat it dear, or it will get cold".

She would never look me straight in the eye, but always turned her gaze away from me, like she was hiding something from me. It worried me a good deal.

I decided that I should have a talk with her about it and said, "sister, do you think summer is beautiful here?"

She said, "all the days that God gives us are beautiful, if we can see it. It's a shame that a simple allergy like hay fever is making your summer hell".

I said, "you're right. But how is it with you these days?"

"My days are all the same sister, all grey and foggy. I'm going to make some cinnamon tea for you now. Eat your food, please".

She was with me until sunset, but we didn't talk very much. I had no desire to talk, and she didn't insist. But what she had said resonated around and around in my head - all my days are grey and foggy. I wish I knew what was in her mind.

That night I went to bed earlier than Farhad. I had an extreme cold and a fever. My mind was unsettled, and I was worried. The sound of the phone ringing woke me up. The clock showed it was only 3:00 am. My heart was thudding when I picked it up, like I was expecting bad news. It was Vahid. I was overcome with fear and concern, and I was in shock. Farhad woke up and he took the phone from my hand and asked Vahid what had happened? He left the room for a moment and then returned and gave me back the phone.

He said, "come, we should go to Roya's house".

"What happened?"

"Get ready."

I was going crazy. I couldn't tolerate it, but Farhad only told me not to worry.

I couldn't stand it any longer and called Vahid back.

"Hello Vahid. What happened, my son?"

He sobbed as he told me, "Aunt come quickly, my mother is dying".

I said, "call an ambulance; we are on our way".

A cold sweat was on my forehead, like death was in front of me and calling me. When we arrived, Roya was in bed. She was struggling to tell me something through her laboured breathing but managed to get out a few words.

"Be like a mother to Vahid".

My god, what was happening?

I turned to Farhad asked, "will she be, okay?"

He said, "her breath smells of death, but have hope …".

www.ingramcontent.com/pod-product-compliance
Lightning Source LLC
Chambersburg PA
CBHW040420100526
44589CB00021B/2771